The Ultimate Path to Jannah

MUFTI ISMAIL MENK
Transcribed and adapted from the lecture
"When The Gates of Jannah Open: Divine Promises for The Righteous"

Published by:

Unit No. E-10-5, Jalan SS 15/4G, Subang Square,
47500 Subang Jaya, Selangor, Malaysia
+603-5612-2407 (office) / +6017-399-7411 (mobile)
info@tertib.press
www.tertib.press
@tertibpress (Facebook & Instagram)

Author	:	Mufti Ismail Menk
Transcriber & Editor	:	Nadiah Aslam
Proofreader	:	Arisha Mohd Affendy
		Hanis Husna Adzhar
Cover designer	:	Abdul Adzim Md Daim
Typesetter	:	Abdul Adzim Md Daim

THE ULTIMATE PATH TO JANNAH

First Edition: December 2024

Perpustakaan Negara Malaysia

Cataloguing-in-Publication Data

A catalogue record for this book is available from the National Library of Malaysia

ISBN: 978-967-2844-43-3 (hardback)

Copyright © Mufti Ismail Menk 2024

All rights reserved.
No part of this publication may be reproduced, distributed, or transmitted in any form or by any means, including photocopying, recording, or other electronic or mechanical methods, without the prior written permission of Tertib Publishing.
Printed in Malaysia.

Contents

Preface	1
Part 1: The Creation of Allah	3
Chapter 1: The Desire to Meet	4
Chapter 2: The Desire to Be Loved	9
Chapter 3: The Desire to Love	14
Chapter 4: The Desire for Worldly Allure	20
Chapter 5: The Almighty Creator	25
Chapter 6: The Kingdom that Never Decreases	32
Chapter 7: Beautiful in the Eyes of Allah	39
Part 2: The Path to *Jannah*	43
Chapter 8: All Eyes on *Jannah*	44
Chapter 9: The Life We Do Not Remember	53
Chapter 10: Death is the Beginning of A New Life	58

Chapter 11: Good Deeds as Bricks for *Jannah*	62
Chapter 12: The Deed of Patience	69
Chapter 13: The Meeting with the Angel of Death	76
Chapter 14: The Realm After Death	90
Chapter 15: Friends and Foes	94
Chapter 16: Good Company	98
Part 3: The Essence of *Jannah*	**104**
Chapter 17: The Gates of *Jannah* and *Jahannam*	105
Chapter 18: The People of *Jahannam* in *Jannah*	111
Chapter 19: The One Who Loves to Meet Allah	115
Chapter 20: Perfection in *Jannah*	122
Chapter 21: Spouses in *Jannah*	127
Chapter 22: The Wish List That Will Not Exist	133

Part 4: Supplications and Acts for the Ultimate Meeting — 137

   Chapter 23: *Du'a'* for the Best Ending — 138

   Chapter 24: *Du'a'* for the Meeting with Allah — 141

   Chapter 25: Seeking Allah's Forgiveness — 146

   Chapter 26: Improving Ourselves — 151

   Chapter 27: Staying Connected to Allah — 154

Ending Remarks — 158

Arabic Glossary — 163

يَوْمِيَّة جَبْهَة الفِرْدَوْس

Preface

Dear readers, assalamu'alaikum waraḥmatullahi wabarakatuh.

The work you are holding within your hands aims to illuminate the path to *Jannah* and explore the profound wisdom behind Allah's creation. Based on a lecture that I delivered some time ago in Malaysia titled "When the Gates of *Jannah* Open: Divine Promises for the Righteous," this book delves into the fundamental desires that Allah Almighty has instilled within us and how they relate to our ultimate goal of attaining Paradise.

Throughout these pages, we will explore the innate human desires to meet others, to love and be loved, and to experience the wonders of this world. We will reflect on how these desires, when properly directed, can lead us closer to our Creator and to the eternal bliss of *Jannah*.

This book is not merely a collection of religious teachings, but a heartfelt invitation to ponder the magnificence of Allah's creation and the incomparable rewards He has prepared for the righteous slaves. We will examine the nature of human relationships, the transient allure of worldly possessions, and the unimaginable beauty of Paradise that awaits the believers.

As we journey through these brief chapters, we will be reminded of our purpose in this life and the importance of cultivating a strong relationship with Allah Almighty. We will learn to appreciate the beauty in ourselves and others as Allah's creation and to align our desires with that which pleases Him, the Lord of one and all.

It is my sincere hope that this book will serve as a source of inspiration, reflection, and guidance for all who seek the path to *Jannah*. May Allah Almighty accept our efforts and grant us all entry into the highest level of *Jannah*, *āmīn*.

PART 1

The Creation of Allah

CHAPTER 1

The Desire to Meet

Dear brothers and sisters, how many of us have people that we look up to?

How many of us have people who we want to meet one day? Be it a reciter of the Qur'an, a speaker, a politician, or anyone else, the fact is we all have at least one person we are desperate to meet one day.

It is true that Allah the Almighty has kept within humankind desires. From among those desires, there are the permissible desires and the prohibited desires. One of the permissible desires is the desire to meet someone.

When I was young, I used to love hearing the imams of Makkah on the radio. Perhaps some might know this radio channel—MW 1548. I used to tune in to this channel to listen to the recitation of the Qur'an and to listen to the *tarawiḥ* prayers during Ramadan. *SubḥānAllāh*, the recitation was beautiful. I used to desire to meet these amazing people one day. I know who they are. I know their names and their ways of recitation. This was during the 1980s and 1981s when I was six or seven years old.

One day, I had the opportunity to go to Makkah with my close one, and we managed to meet the imams and the reciters that we have been dreaming of meeting, *subḥānAllāh*. There were still some people that we yearned to see, but unfortunately did not manage to. And we can only say, "Oh I'm going to meet them *inshā'Allāh* since I'm already here,"

And so, these kinds of situations happen, these kinds of desires are felt. We experience this kind of desire—wanting to meet someone; to greet them, to say a word to them, to have a conversation with them and so on. That is, indeed, something beautiful because that is the way Allah the Almighty has created us.

There will be some people whom we will never have the chance to meet, even though we are desperate. If there is a chance, if Allah gives us the chance, perhaps *inshā'Allāh* we will meet them in the Hereafter. Pray to Allah and ask Him, "O' Allah, I couldn't meet so-and-so in the *dunya*. So, allow me to meet them in the Hereafter." However, there is something that we have to be careful of here, my dear brothers and sisters. We have to be careful about the kinds of people we want to meet.

We should always pray to want to meet good people. If we pray to, perhaps, meet someone who is so sinful and so astray from the path of Allah—where do we think we will meet them? Where will we have the meeting with them in the Hereafter?

Have you thought of this, dear brothers and sisters?

I know a few names of people who are far off the *deen*. They are known, unfortunately, for doing sinful acts—indulging in the prohibitions, showing off their bodies and so on. And so, are we really going to pray to Allah to allow us to meet them in the *akhirah*—in *Jahannam*? Are we going to pray for that? No, of course not.

Therefore, have this mindset: If we meet the people we want to meet, that is okay, and if we do not get to meet them, it is okay as well. Trust me, dear brothers and sisters. We do not want to have a meeting with those kinds of people in the *akhirah* at a place that we do not even want to be in close vicinity—Hellfire.

Additionally, this mindset should not only be applied for the Hereafter but also to the *dunya* as well. When we have to go to a good place in the *dunya* to meet someone, *inshā'Allāh*, it means that they are good people. On the other hand, if we have to go to a club or pub, or a place where they are doing clandestine activities, or dirty things to meet someone, then it probably indicates that the person is at the sinful level. May Allah the Almighty protect us. May Allah the Almighty strengthen us.

It is better to
sit alone than
in company with
the bad;

and it is better
still to sit with the
good ones than to
be alone

CHAPTER 2

The Desire to Be Loved

Let us delve into the next desire that Allah the Almighty has created within us: the desire to be loved.

We all want to be loved. I too want to be loved.

I want someone to say to me, "You're looking good today." 😊

I also want someone to tell me, "You're looking good today." 😎

I also want someone to say to me, "Muah! You're looking so good today." 😗

These are the different ways of saying to someone how good they are looking. These expressions depend on who we are talking to. Sometimes, our expressions and tone of voice change depending on who we are talking to.

For instance, if we are talking to a child, we will show a different type of affection as compared to the one we show to our friends and peers. Additionally, our response to hearing a compliment also differs, depending on who we receive the compliment from.

Basically, we all have this desire to be loved—to be appreciated. We feel like we could conquer the world simply because those around us are empowering us and loving us in the right way.

That is why parents must always pay heed to the way they communicate and talk with their children. When parents are talking to their children, when they are correcting or reprimanding them—they must not use degrading words that belittle them and destroy their confidence. And so, when parents want to correct and reprimand their children, they must first and foremost know how to do it correctly.

This is not only applied to our own children but to all other children as well, including people whom we work with. When we want to correct someone, we must not use belittling words. Empower them and say,

"I love you, but I need to tell you that this thing needs to change. But I love you."

The other day, one of my children made a mistake. She did something that she was not supposed to do. I told her that she had to go to the naughty corner for an hour. An hour is a long time for the child. And so, my daughter was just staring and looking at me, which wrenched my heart. I told her, "I love you so much, but you have to go to the corner and think about what you did." She was very sad. She cried a bit and then she went to the corner as I was quite firm about it. I did not let the whole hour pass because obviously, an hour is too much. I asked her after a while, "Have you thought about it? Was it right what you did?" She said, "No. It was wrong." And so, I let her go. After she realised and thought about her actions, I let her leave the naughty corner.

The reason why I opted for this method is because I do not want to belittle my children. I do not want to make them feel small because they also need to be loved. Children look up to their parents. The minute the parent gives a signal that indicates they do not love them, it will then shatter them. To them it is the end of their lives—the end of their world. Why? Because the parents are the main people in their lives—they are the centre of their lives.

The minute the child gets a signal from their mother or father that they do not love them—then that is it. It will shatter them. They might get into habits that are far from right. May Allah Almighty strengthen our children and grant us goodness, *āmīn*.

When a Muslim has love for their fellow Muslims for the sake of Allah, they should let them know of this love.

CHAPTER 3

The Desire to Love

Let us now explore the desire to love.

We all have within us the trait of loving—giving love to people. We love and we want to be loved as well. This is something amazing, *subḥānAllāh*.

When we love someone, we normally love them for different reasons. Sometimes, we love someone because they are a part of our family. For instance, our children, our spouses, our parents, our siblings and our relatives. We love them because they are connected to us. Allah created that connection.

Spouses

When it comes to our spouses, Allah (s.w.t.) has said in the Qur'an:

$$\text{وَمِنْ ءَايَٰتِهِۦٓ أَنْ خَلَقَ لَكُم مِّنْ أَنفُسِكُمْ أَزْوَٰجًا لِّتَسْكُنُوٓا۟ إِلَيْهَا وَجَعَلَ بَيْنَكُم مَّوَدَّةً وَرَحْمَةً ۚ إِنَّ فِى ذَٰلِكَ لَءَايَٰتٍ لِّقَوْمٍ يَتَفَكَّرُونَ ۝}$$

And of His signs is that He created for you from yourselves mates that you may find tranquillity in them; and He placed between you affection and mercy. Indeed in that are signs for a people who give thought.

(Qur'an, ar-Rum, 30:21)

From Allah's signs, He has created for us spouses from ourselves, and He (s.w.t.) has placed between us *mawaddah* and *raḥmah*.

In the verse above, Allah (s.w.t.) speaks about the qualities that He will place within the heart of a genuine spouse, which are *mawaddah* or compassion, and *raḥmah* or mercy. And so, as soon as we get married, there is a special connection—compassion and mercy. If we do not feel any special connection, then it is a problem.

> *If it is not present, then perhaps the seed that has been sown is haram.*
>
> *If it is not present, then perhaps the seed that has been sown is in the disobedience to Allah.*

Thus, we need to feel that connection more than anything else. We need to feel mercy towards our spouses. We need to make sure that no harm comes to them. We need to make sure we love them abundantly. They are the coolness of our eyes. May Allah grant us good spouses, *āmīn*.

In essence, that is the love Allah has created between spouses. And so, when we want to get married, do it the right way. Do not do it the wrong way. Look for good qualities in people. Do not just look for appearances because when we just concentrate on appearances, they will end up deceiving us. We would not be able to look at those appearances longer than we initially thought. After some time of looking at them, suddenly they will change. The face will start to change and have all these marks, blemishes, lines, creases and wrinkles. All these have nothing to do with love. *SubḥānAllāh*, it has nothing to do with that.

As time goes by, spouses should be getting closer and closer to each other. That is the *deen* of Allah. Just look at how amazing it is that Allah has created *mawaddah* and *raḥmah* in the heart, *subḥānAllāh*.

Children

On the other hand, when it comes to our children, there is an automatic love. Why? Because they are our own, they are our child. If we are a believer of Allah, we will love our children and that love is a natural love. We might dislike some of their deeds and actions, but we will still love them despite all of that.

There are some people who, unfortunately, have children who are not on the *deen* of Allah. And so, the parents do not love the fact that their children are not on the *deen* but they still love them. The natural love parents have towards their children will still be present and nobody can take that away from them.

Let me give another example. Perhaps we have

reverted to Islam, however, our mother has not. We love her to bits and pieces and that is the natural love we have for her. However, at the same time, we dislike the fact that she does not believe in Allah.

Can you see the difference, dear brothers and sisters?

The Prophet Muḥammad (s.a.w.) loved his uncle, Abu Ṭalib so much even though he was not a believer. Likewise with Abu Ṭalib. He loved his nephew so much that he defended him (s.a.w.) from the idol worshippers, from the disbelievers. The love they both had was overflowing. The Prophet (s.a.w.) loved his uncle so much but he (s.a.w.) did not like the fact that his uncle was not a believer.

In a nutshell, this is the desire for love that we have. This is Allah's creation. Allah the Almighty has placed within the heart love and connection. *SubḥānAllāh*.

Learn enough about your lineage to maintain the ties of kinship.

For indeed keeping the ties of kinship encourages affection among the relatives, increases the wealth, and increases the lifespan

CHAPTER 4

The Desire for Worldly Allure

All of us desire things. We desire to have an amazing car, we desire to have the latest designer clothes, we desire to have the latest technology, we desire to go to places and more.

Once, I was driving to the venue of a lecture in an amazing car. And so, I thought to myself that everyone must have a favourite car or dream car. If I were to ask people about their favourite car, they would probably say Toyota but the ones who will be the most excited in answering this question will be those who have yet to have a driver's license—children. They are the most excited when it comes to this question. They are the ones who are looking forward to the day they can drive a Lamborghini.

By the way, Malaysians should answer this question with Proton. If it were me, I would have said Proton. Even though I might not like one or two things about the Proton car, the idea is that, *inshā'Allāh*, it will change and improve someday. It is still a lovely car and a big achievement for the country. May Allah grant us goodness.

Back to the topic, everyone also has a place or destination that they want to go to. For instance, Penang, Langkawi, Bali, Nigeria and more. For some people, it is their dream to see the Northern Lights, so they want to go to the place where they can see it. And so, these are some of the dream destinations of some of us. The question now is, will we get there? Will we be able to fulfil our dreams of going there? Will we be able to see the Northern Lights someday? *Wallāhi*, I do not know, dear brothers and sisters. Maybe we will and maybe we will not. However, I do know something beautiful, something amazing; We like places that are natural creations of Allah, a natural wonder.

The majority of the time we like a place is because of its natural scenery. The majority of the time we like the place because it has an ocean, sea, beautiful water, beautiful weather and scenery. In essence, most of the holiday destinations that amaze and wow us are natural places. Very few places without these things—greenery, mountains, sea—attract us. Only sometimes we are attracted to places of development for shopping and just to see how things have changed. Other than that, it is very rare for us to make malls our dream destinations.

Additionally, when we go shopping, we usually go to the malls that have everything there—designer clothes, technology, high-end brands and so on—but we do not have the money to buy the things. And so, consequently, what do we end up doing? Window shopping.

We will be looking around at the latest clothes and technology whilst saying, "*Inshā'Allāh* I will get that one day," hence, window shopping. We will roam around whilst saying, "*Inshā'Allāh* I will get that Rolex watch soon," "*Inshā'Allāh* I will get that S24 phone one day." *Wallāhi* dear brothers and sisters, by the time we come back to the place to buy the S24, the S27 will be released and be the trending item. Would we then want to get the S24 or S27? We would want the latest items.

This is not only for technology but everything else

as well. When we are able to buy the items that we want, they would not be trending anymore. As time passes, the items will be replaced with new things, which would be the trending items. Would we really want them then—the things that we once wanted instead of the latest items?

Firstly, we would enjoy window shopping by uttering, "*Mashā'Allāh*," and then, "*Inshā'Allāh*," meaning one day, we would return and get it. However, as I mentioned, by the time we come back, there will be something else that is trending. The item that we wanted will no longer be something that we want. Does this not happen to us, dear brothers and sisters? It does.

In essence, we have within us these desires to want the latest technology, the latest car and the desires to want to go to places. These things make us happy. The question now is who is the one who made these things that give us joy? Who is the Creator of everything? Who is the Creator of the nature that we are attracted to? Who is the Creator of the people we love? Who is the Creator of the nature we love—the places that have the greenery, the Northern lights, the dream destinations? It is Allah the Almighty.

He is Allah: the Creator, the Inventor, the Shaper.

He alone has the Most Beautiful Names.

Whatever is in the heavens and the earth constantly glorifies Him.

And He is the Almighty, All-Wise.

CHAPTER 5

The Almighty Creator

Have we ever pondered while looking at the people we love, the things we cherish and the natural wonder around us, about who the Creator of all these is?

Who is the Creator of all things? It is Allah the Glorious and Majestic.

When we see and ponder about the creation of Allah, we are always in awe. Have we then taken a moment to wonder how amazing the Creator Himself?

$$\text{هَٰذَا خَلْقُ ٱللَّهِ فَأَرُونِى مَاذَا خَلَقَ ٱلَّذِينَ مِن دُونِهِۦ ۚ بَلِ ٱلظَّٰلِمُونَ فِى ضَلَٰلٍ مُّبِينٍ ﴿١١﴾}$$

This is the creation of Allah. So show Me what those other than Him have created. Rather, the wrongdoers are in clear error.

(Qur'an, Luqman, 31:11)

All that we see and love is by Allah the Almighty. This is the creation of Allah. Nothing is created except by Him (s.w.t.).

When we look into our eyes and see a megapixel without any fine-tuning, without the need to focus or auto-focus, it is something amazing, is it not? Why is it so amazing? Because it is the creation of Allah (s.w.t.). *Mashā'Allāh*, the way we walk, the way we hear in such a beautiful way without attaching any apparatus is incredible. The way our heart beats is remarkable. Imagine watching our heart beat 136,000 times a day through a scan. Will we not ponder or believe for a moment that there is a Creator to all of these? We will.

Just imagine, if His creation is already wowing us, then how much more remarkable would the Creator be? These kinds of thoughts and questions are absolutely amazing, and the believer will most definitely ask and ponder about it.

The Earth is supposed to be cheap in the eyes of Allah, but we are already so amazed and impressed by it. So imagine the Creator—imagine *Jannah*, the place that He has built for the dwellers of *Jannah*.

I do know that Dr. Muhammad Salah and Shaykh Wael Ibrahim have touched this hadith in their books as well—*The Celestial Beauty of Jannah* and *The Blueprint for A House in Jannah*—respectively. However, it is a point that I would like to mention once again to emphasise its importance. Allah the Almighty told us that there is something unique about the eternal abode of bliss when we get there *inshāʾAllāh*. What do we think we will get and find in *Jannah*? Nothing that we have ever imagined.

Did you know that anything that has crossed our mind is not there?

Did you know that anything that we see in this life is not there?

Did you know that anything we heard about Jannah is not there?

Why? Because it is the place that surpasses all imagination.

It is mentioned in the following hadith that what will be in *Jannah* is beyond our imagination:

Narrated Abu Hurayrah:

> The Prophet (s.a.w.) said, "Allah said, 'I have prepared for My pious worshippers such things as no eye has ever seen, no ear has ever heard of, and nobody has ever thought of. All that is reserved, besides which, all that you have seen, is nothing.'" Then he recited: "No soul knows what is kept hidden (in reserve) for them of joy as a reward for what they used to do (Qur'an, as-Sajdah, 32:17)."
>
> (Ṣaḥīḥ al-Bukhari 4780)

Jannah surpasses all imaginations. It is a place that is beyond our imagination and cannot be fathomed.

For instance, the person who we know in the *dunya*, will be in *Jannah* in a different way, they will not be in the way we see them. Meaning, the people whom we know in this *dunya*, will perhaps appear differently in *Jannah*. They will be there in *Jannah*, but they are different as compared to how we know them; even spouses. Our spouses will be in *Jannah* with us *inshāʾAllāh*.

$$ ٱدْخُلُوا۟ ٱلْجَنَّةَ أَنتُمْ وَأَزْوَٰجُكُمْ تُحْبَرُونَ ۝ $$

Enter Paradise, you and your kinds, delighted.

(Qurʾan, az-Zukhruf, 43:70)

However, some people have mentioned to me that they would rather not go to *Jannah* if their spouse is there. Why? Because they have been through so many ordeals, challenges and have led a difficult life because of their spouse. And so, they would rather be with someone else, with someone who will give them peace and tranquillity. However, hold this thought first brothers and sisters, and instead, just focus on the path to getting to *Jannah*.

Wait a moment and just think of getting there first. Get to *Jannah* and see what there really is. We will be surprised when we are in *Jannah*. It will be different from this life. The people will be different. It is a place where all wishes come true. It is a place where there will only be peace and everlasting happiness. What we will get there is beyond any imagination. Therefore, just focus on getting to *Jannah* first.

Allah is the **Creator** of all things, and He is the **Maintainer** of everything.

To Him belong the keys of the **treasuries** of the **heavens** and the **earth**.

As for those who **rejected** the **signs** of Allah, it is they who will be the **true losers**.

CHAPTER 6

The Kingdom that Never Decreases

Allah the Almighty is so powerful.

Allah the Almighty tells us in the Qur'an that He has created this earth and He has created mankind, jinn and other creations:

$$\text{وَمَا خَلَقْتُ ٱلْجِنَّ وَٱلْإِنسَ إِلَّا لِيَعْبُدُونِ ۝}$$

And I did not create the *jinn* and mankind except to worship Me.

(Qur'an, adh-Dhariyat, 51:56)

We will never know the majority of the creation of Allah.

Let me give an example. How many of us live in an area where there is a coast, beach, river, or sea? When we go scuba diving or snorkelling, we will see creatures that we never knew existed. Do we know how many species there are in the ocean? It is uncountable. Millions is based on what we have seen. There is much more that we have not seen and discovered. Every day there is always a new discovery.

Likewise about the galaxy as well. Do we know how many planets there are? No. No one knows the exact number. There is so much yet to be discovered. With the latest technology, the James Webb telescope, people are now discovering new planets, humongous planets, planets bigger than anything they have ever seen. And these discoveries keep increasing as every single day passes by. One might wonder when these new discoveries will reach their end—when will everything be discovered? Now that is the creation of Allah, *subḥānAllāh*.

Dear brothers and sisters, do you know what Allah has said about His Bounties and His Kingdom? It is something that will never decrease. Allah the Almighty mentions to us in Hadith Qudsi, "O' son of Adam, if the first of you and the last of you, and the first of *jinn* kind and the last of *jinn* kind—if all of you had to ask me for everything that you ever wanted, and I gave every one of mankind every single thing they desired for; and every *jinn* kind, from the beginning of *jinn* kind to the end of *jinn* kind—every single thing they desired. It would not be displaced from my Kingdom except that which is displaced when the needle is put into the ocean and lifted."

SubḥānAllāh. That is Allah, dear brothers and sisters:

On the authority of Abu Dharr al-Ghifari (r.a.) from the Prophet (s.a.w.) is that among the sayings he relates from his Lord (s.w.t.) is that He said:

> O' My servants, I have forbidden oppression for Myself and have made it forbidden amongst you, so do not oppress one another. O' My servants, all of you are astray except for those I have guided, so seek guidance of Me and I shall guide you. O' My servants, all of you are hungry except for those I have fed, so seek food of Me and I shall feed you. O' My servants, all of you are naked except for

those I have clothed, so seek clothing of Me and I shall clothe you. O' My servants, you sin by night and by day, and I forgive all sins, so seek forgiveness of Me and I shall forgive you. O' My servants, you will not attain harming Me so as to harm Me, and will not attain benefitting Me so as to benefit Me. O' My servants, were the first of you and the last of you, the human of you and the *jinn* of you to be as pious as the most pious heart of any one man of you, that would not increase My kingdom in anything. O' My servants, were the first of you and the last of you, the human of you and the *jinn* of you to be as wicked as the most wicked heart of any one man of you, that would not decrease My kingdom in anything. O' My servants, were the first of you and the last of you, the human of you and the *jinn* of you to rise up in one place and make a request of Me, and were I to give everyone what he requested, that would not decrease what I have, any more that a needle decreases the sea if put into it. O' My servants, it is but your deeds that I reckon up for you and then recompense you for, so let him who finds good, praise Allah, and let him who finds other than that, blame no one but himself. It was related by Muslim (also by at-Tirmidhi and Ibn Majah).

(Hadith 17, 40 Hadith Qudsi)

What do we want, brothers and sisters? We usually want billions and trillions of things. Allah mentions in the hadith above that if He (s.w.t.) were to give every single mankind and *jinn* kind anything and everything they wanted, it would not reduce His (s.w.t.) Kingdom at all. And this is not only about the current population. It encompasses every single human kind and *jinn* kind from the very beginning of existence. All the things every single person has received are nothing to Allah—it does not affect His Kingdom, it does not decrease His Kingdom.

There are just so many creations we do not know who have received the bounties of Allah. There is more than what meets the eye. We only know some of the things, like the things we see, the things on Earth.

As mentioned further in the above hadith when we came unto Earth, it is through Allah's mercy and bounties we were protected; such that we were born unclothed, then were quickly covered by Allah's will. And so, when we are leaving this *dunya*, we will be covered with a shroud as an honour by Allah's will. May Allah make it easy for all of us on that day. May Allah make it easy on the day we meet death.

Indeed, the kingdom of the heavens and the earth belongs solely to Allah,

and there is no guardian or helper for you besides Him

CHAPTER 7

Beautiful in the Eyes of Allah

Dear brothers and sisters, Allah has created us all beautifully. In the eyes of Allah, we are in the finest state.

Sometimes, when we look at people, we think and say, "*Mashā'Allāh*, so beautiful." Usually, women do this a lot. Additionally, the majority of the time women are quite obsessed with their skin. And so, they would put makeup on to look like they have flawless skin. Am I right?

Sometimes, they have good skin but they spoil it with makeup. Dear brothers and sisters, our skin is beautiful. We do not need any makeup. Allah has already made us beautiful in advance, *mashā'Allāh*.

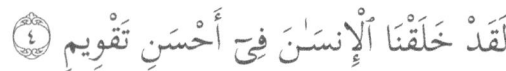

We have certainly created man in the best of stature.

(Qur'an, at-Tin, 95:4)

It is true that we are only fully liberated once we love ourselves the exact way Allah has made us. So, love ourselves. Love our complexion, love our nose, love our hair, love our eyes—love the way Allah has made us. We are special in the eyes of Allah.

It is okay to not be special in the eyes of others, because in the eyes of Allah, we are, and that is of the utmost importance. When we embody and embrace this, we will then be fully liberated.

However, the minute we start saying things about what we dislike about ourselves, we will then end up not liking anything about ourselves. We will find problems with everything that we have. We will find problems even with the littlest of hair that we have like our eyelashes and eyebrows.

We will find a problem with our lips. We want it to be a millimetre more plump and then we will end up doing something that will make it appear that way.

Wallāhi, we will end up looking like a ghost when we alter the way we have already been made.

In essence, to be liberated is to love ourselves the way Allah has created us. Do not be enslaved to the thoughts that we are not beautiful and end up altering it. Leave our features the way they are, leave our complexion the way it is and love ourselves the way Allah has created us.

In the eyes of Allah you are beautiful.

You have been created in the best of form.

You have been created beautifully.

Therefore love yourself and be liberated.

Do not chain yourself to the thoughts that you are not beautiful.

PART 2

The Path to *Jannah*

CHAPTER 8

All Eyes on *Jannah*

Dear brothers and sisters, I would like to teach you something.

I know that we are all excited about what we will get in *Jannah inshā'Allāh*. However, do not let that excitement make us lose focus on *Jannah*—do not let it make us lose the road to *Jannah*, do not let it make us lose our path to *Jannah*. Work towards getting to the eternal abode of bliss, that is all. Everything else shall be by the way. Why? Because *shaytan* has a big plan for us and that is making us lose *Jannah*.

In order for *shaytan* to make us lose our *Jannah*, he will start making us fight about what we will get there and what we will not. He will start casting doubts and whispers into our minds and hearts to misguide us from the path to *Jannah*. Consequently, when *shaytan* does that, and we allow ourselves to fight about those things—we will lose our path and will not get to *Jannah*.

For instance, if we are busy arguing whether or not our pets—cats and dogs—will be in *Jannah* and miss our prayers because of it, then that means we are going astray. If we end up in a state where we are not dressing properly, we are listening and watching things that we are not supposed to, we are doing things that we are not supposed to and are not doing things that we are supposed to do—it means those thoughts and doubts are already making us lose our *Jannah*. It is taking us away from the path of *Jannah*.

If we are not doing the things that we are supposed to do, we are losing focus on *Jannah*. Let me give a few more examples. We have never been to *hajj* but we can afford it. We did not give our *zakah* when we were supposed to. We did not fast much in Ramadan even though we were supposed to. We do not pray five times a day even though we are supposed to. Here we are fighting about the things that we will have or not in *Jannah*, about whether our cats and dogs will be in *Jannah* and it made us lose our focus. I am not implying that our cats and dogs will not be in *Jannah*. I am just saying that the goal and the focus is to just get to *Jannah*, to do the things that we are supposed to do to get to *Jannah*. Focus on getting to *Jannah* first. Do not think about what we will have or will not have there.

It is reported in a *ṣaḥīḥ* hadith that the last person to enter *Jannah* will receive ten times more than what the heavens and the earth hold. This is meant in a unique way whereby it does not mean the things that were on Earth, but something more extraordinary and breathtaking, something that is beyond imagination:

It was narrated from 'Abdullah bin Mas'ud that the Messenger of Allah (s.a.w.) said:

> "I know the last of the people of Hell who will be brought forth from it, and the last of the people of Paradise to be admitted to Paradise. (It is) a man who will emerge from Hell crawling, and it will be said to him: 'Go and enter Paradise.' He will come to it and it will be made to appear to him as if it is full. Allah will say: 'Go and enter Paradise.' He

will come to it and it will appear to him as if it is full. So he will say: 'O' Lord, I found it full.' Allah will say: 'Go and enter Paradise.' He will come to it and it will be made to appear to him as if it is full. So he will say: 'O' Lord, I found it full.' Allah will say: 'Go and enter Paradise, for you will have the like of the world and ten times more, or you will have ten times the like of the world.' He will say: 'Are You mocking me, or are You laughing at me, when You are the Sovereign?'" He said: "And I saw the Messenger of Allah (s.a.w.) smiling so broadly that his molar teeth could be seen." And he used to say: "This is the lowest of the people of Paradise in status."

(Sunan ibn Majah 4339)

Furthermore, in *Jannah* we will all have our own gardens. *SubḥānAllāh*, each of us will have our own place in *Jannah*:

وَعَدَ ٱللَّهُ ٱلْمُؤْمِنِينَ وَٱلْمُؤْمِنَٰتِ جَنَّٰتٍ تَجْرِى مِن تَحْتِهَا ٱلْأَنْهَٰرُ خَٰلِدِينَ فِيهَا

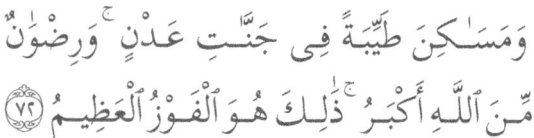

Allah has promised the believing men and believing women gardens beneath which rivers flow, wherein they abide eternally, and pleasant dwellings in gardens of perpetual residence; but approval from Allah is greater. It is that which is the great attainment.

(Qur'an, at-Tawbah, 9:72)

When we enter *Jannah* we will be so impressed. We will be so amazed that at the gates of *Jannah*, we will just be standing and being amazed that we forget to enter it. We are in joy just looking at *Jannah* and forget to enter it.

Can you imagine this, dear brothers and sisters? *SubḥānAllāh*.

There is no place on this Earth that we would enter and then stop and look at it for a year or so. No. We might stop a few minutes and say, "*Mashā'Allāh*," but that is it. After a few hours or after a few days at a holiday destination, we will get bored. All the places that I mentioned in Chapter 4 pertaining to the dream destinations are beautiful places but they are not worth living for an eternity no matter their beauty. There is no holiday resort or destination that we will enjoy forever. We would want to go back home. We need our family and people. We need to be where Allah made us and brought us to this Earth. The place where we are born and raised is the place that we will always be connected to somehow. Even if we shift countries and become a citizen of another nation elsewhere—home is home.

Do you not agree, dear brothers and sisters?

Home will always be home. No place smells and feels like the *kampung* (village). It has a unique scent, does it not? We go there and we feel that all of our stress is gone. We can smell whatever it is there, whether it is the agriculture, plantation, the animals, the cows and so on. Each one's *kampung* is dear to them.

Basically, we need to prepare ourselves to go to *Jannah*. We need to focus on **going** to *Jannah* more than focusing on **what** we are going to get in there. I am not saying that it is wrong to ask what we will get in *Jannah*. We can ask about it but the main attention is being on the path to the eternal abode of bliss. We can get the answers about the things in *Jannah* from the Qur'an and the hadith. However, we must just stop there. Whatever has been said in the Qur'an and hadith pertaining to *Jannah*, take that as an answer and just stop there. Do not try to know more.

In essence, get to *Jannah* first and just focus on getting there. When we get there, we will have whatever we want, *inshā'Allāh*. The keyword is basically when we are there. We do not have to decide and finalise here in this *dunya* what we want in *Jannah*. Therefore have this mindset: *Inshā'Allāh* whatever we want, Allah will give it to us when we are in *Jannah*. That is more important than saying, "I need this and I need that."

Before we end this chapter, I would like to give an example. I mentioned in Chapter 4 about desiring the latest items, the S24 phone for instance. If Allah gave us the S24 after two years, we would not appreciate it. Why? Because it is something that we no longer want. Why? Because after a year or two it has become something that is irrelevant to us as there is something else that is newer and trendier. However, *Jannah* is not like that. Just wait until we get to see the "S *Jannah*" dear brothers and sisters. When we get *Jannah*, we would not want anything else at all. We probably would not even remember anything that was on this Earth and, *inshā'Allāh*, I will be touching on this in the next chapter.

Allah has promised the believing men and believing women gardens beneath which rivers flow, wherein they abide eternally, and pleasant dwellings in gardens of perpetual residence; but approval from Allah is greater. It is that which is the great attainment.

CHAPTER 9

The Life We Do Not Remember

I mentioned in the previous chapter that when we get to the Hereafter, we will probably not remember life on Earth. Let me give an example pertaining to this matter which is the life we had in the womb of our mother.

Dear brothers and sisters, do we remember being in the wombs of our mothers? Do we remember the day we were born? Do we remember crying when we came into this *dunya*? No. None of us remember the life we had in the wombs of our mothers and that is a fact. Why?

It is also a fact that we were there. We were there for nine months. We drank and ate there; we were fed in a unique way which was through the umbilical cord. We enjoyed our time there, in the warm embrace of our mother and we were safe from external harm. We experienced all of these things but we do not remember them. When we came into existence, to this *dunya*, we did not remember a single thing. Why? Because Allah does not want us to remember it. And so, who knows if the same thing will happen again or not when we cross from this *dunya* to the Hereafter?

Furthermore, nowadays there is evidence that a child was in the womb. People take videos and pictures of the child's scan and their action of kicking in the womb. Later, the parents show the videos of children kicking in the womb and they probably wonder and ask, "Is that really me? Are you sure that is me kicking? I don't remember a thing." The parents will say, "Of course it's you. Who do you expect it to be? Did you think we swap babies or something?"

Additionally, the technology is so advanced to the point we can now see a 3D image of the baby. The parents can see the face of their child before they are even born whilst thinking about whom the baby looks like more—the mother or the father. Trust me, dear brothers and sisters, the baby looks like both of the parents. It keeps changing every day and when they grow up, perhaps then they look like one of them more. But the fact is they have features from all sides. That is Allah's way.

In a nutshell, even with all this evidence, we will still not remember. And so, if we cannot even remember the life we had in the womb of our mother, then do we really reckon we will remember the *dunya* life in the Hereafter? It is quite possible that we will not remember everything but there might be a few things that we will remember. We as believers must follow the text, the revelation, the Qur'an. It is mentioned that we will remember certain things but it is that which only Allah wants us to remember. That is what has been said by Allah (s.w.t.).

وَأَقْبَلَ بَعْضُهُمْ عَلَىٰ بَعْضٍ يَتَسَآءَلُونَ ۝ قَالُوٓاْ إِنَّا كُنَّا قَبْلُ فِيٓ أَهْلِنَا مُشْفِقِينَ ۝ فَمَنَّ ٱللَّهُ عَلَيْنَا وَوَقَىٰنَا

And they will approach one another, inquiring of each other. They will say, "Indeed, we were previously among our people fearful [of displeasing Allah]. So Allah conferred favour upon us and protected us from the punishment of the Scorching Fire. Indeed, we used to supplicate Him before. Indeed, it is He who is the Beneficent, the Merciful."

(Qur'an, aṭ-Ṭur, 52:25-28)

Allah has brought you forth from your mothers' wombs when you knew nothing, and He made for you ears, eyes and hearts, so that you may be grateful.

CHAPTER 10

Death is the Beginning of A New Life

Dear readers, I would like to ask you a question: Where do you want to go? Do you want to go to *Jannah*? Many would immediately give "Yes" as the answer because we all want to go to *Jannah*.

Let me ask another question. Are you ready to die? Many would hesitate to answer this question. However dear readers, how will we get to *Jannah* then? How will we get to *Jannah* if we do not die first?

It's like saying that we want to go to Malaysia but we do not want to get onto an aeroplane. How are we going to get to Malaysia then? Please do not say, "*Inshā'Allāh* one day I will be there somehow." How?

Allah says in the Qur'an:

$$\text{ثُمَّ إِنَّكُم بَعْدَ ذَٰلِكَ لَمَيِّتُونَ ۝ ثُمَّ إِنَّكُمْ يَوْمَ الْقِيَامَةِ تُبْعَثُونَ ۝}$$

Then indeed, after that you are to die. Then indeed you, on the Day of Resurrection, will be resurrected.

(Qur'an, al-Mu'minun, 23:15-16)

Indeed we will all die. Afterwards, we will be resurrected on the Day of Judgement and our deeds and actions will be weighed. If we have more good deeds, *inshā'Allāh*, Allah the Almighty will bestow upon us His mercy and will allow us to enter *Jannah*. It is only through the mercy of Allah we will enter the eternal bliss.

In essence, we all want to go to *Jannah* but in order for that to happen we have to first die. And so, death is actually the beginning of a different life altogether—a life that will be everlasting, a life that will be mind-blowing as the believers enter a territory that is beyond imagination. When we see what Allah has prepared for us in *Jannah*, we will be astonished.

Allāhu Akbar. If we are already impressed by the dirt of this *dunya*, imagine what we will feel when we get to *Jannah inshā'Allāh*. Imagine as well, meeting Allah the Almighty. Imagine meeting our Maker, the Creator of all creation, the One who created *Jannah*, the One who created everything in *Jannah*. *SubḥānAllāh*. Imagine how it will be when we meet Him (s.w.t.). We should look forward to that day.

Death is not the end.

It is the start of a beautiful life for the one who lived for Allah.

CHAPTER 11

Good Deeds as Bricks for *Jannah*

As I mentioned in the previous chapter, after death will be the Day of Judgement, the day we will be resurrected and judged based on our good deeds and actions.

Therefore do good deeds. When we think and want to do bad deeds, remember this, and tell ourselves this: "O' Allah, I am going to stay away from this only because it is displeasing to You."

'Abdullah bin 'Umar (r.a.) reported: The Messenger of Allah (s.a.w.) used to supplicate thus:

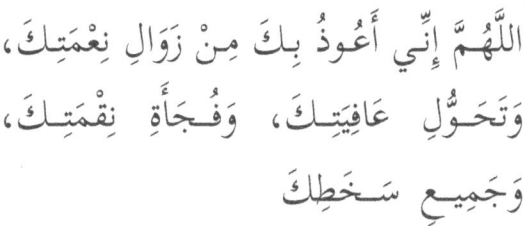

"Allāhumma innī a'ūdhu bika min zawāli ni'matika, wa taḥawwuli 'āfiyatika, wa fujā'ati niqmatika, wa jamī'i sakhatika."

(O' Allah, I seek refuge in You against the declining of Your favours, passing of safety, the suddenness of Your punishment and all that which displeases You)."

(Riyaḍ aṣ-Ṣaliḥin 1478)

If we have fallen into sin, then say this: "O' Allah, forgive me. My human nature made me fall into this sin. I do not want to do it out of defiance to you. I fell into sin because of my *nafs* and *shayṭan*. O' Allah forgive me." *Inshā'Allāh* Allah will forgive us:

Narrated Abu Hurayrah:

I heard the Prophet (s.a.w.) saying, "If somebody commits a sin and then says, 'O' my Lord! I have sinned, please forgive me!'

and his Lord says, 'My slave has known that he has a Lord Who forgives sins and punishes for it, I therefore have forgiven My slave (his sins).' Then he remains without committing any sin for a while and then again commits another sin and says, 'O' my Lord, I have committed another sin, please forgive me,' and Allah says, 'My slave has known that he has a Lord Who forgives sins and punishes for it, I therefore have forgiven My slave (his sin). Then he remains without committing any other sin for a while and then commits another sin (for the third time) and says, 'O' my Lord, I have committed another sin, please forgive me,' and Allah says, 'My slave has known that he has a Lord Who forgives sins and punishes for it I therefore have forgiven My slave (his sin), he can do whatever he likes.'"

(Ṣaḥīḥ al-Bukhari 7507)

Allah says we are forgiven *inshā'Allāh*. If we repent and seek His (s.w.t.) forgiveness, *inshā'Allāh* we will be forgiven. Why should we always seek His (s.w.t.) forgiveness? Because we need it.

Allah does not need our obedience nor is

He affected by our sins. But we are affected. We need Allah's forgiveness in order to go into *Jannah*. Therefore, we must obey Allah and ask for His forgiveness and mercy. We must obey Him (s.w.t.) and do good deeds.

I want to give an example: There is an owner of a building who owns 200 apartments and we want to buy a house. In order to buy the house, we need to work hard to earn the money for it. However, if we are going to eat out every day and not spend our money wisely, then we will not be able to save money for the house. Consequently, when the time comes for us to pay the instalments, we will be unable to pay it and this means we are in big trouble. Similarly, we are paying for our *Jannah*.

What are our instalments for *Jannah*? Our good deeds, our daily prayers, *dhikr*, *ṣadaqah* and more. What are we paying these instalments for? For the day we will meet Allah (s.w.t.):

يَٰٓأَيُّهَا ٱلَّذِينَ ءَامَنُوا۟ ٱتَّقُوا۟ ٱللَّهَ وَلْتَنظُرْ نَفْسٌ مَّا قَدَّمَتْ لِغَدٍ ۖ وَٱتَّقُوا۟ ٱللَّهَ ۚ إِنَّ ٱللَّهَ خَبِيرٌۢ بِمَا تَعْمَلُونَ ﴿١٨﴾

> O' you who have believed, fear Allah. And let every soul look to what it has put forth for tomorrow—and fear Allah. Indeed, Allah is Aware of what you do.
>
> (Qur'an, al-Ḥashr, 59:18)

O' you who believe, be conscious of Allah. Develop the correct relationship with Him (s.w.t.) and look into what we have prepared for tomorrow (the Hereafter).

What have we prepared for our tomorrow—the Hereafter? What have we prepared for the day we are going to meet Allah? Are we going to present our good deeds or bad deeds on the Day of Resurrection? If we have bad deeds, seek Allah's forgiveness. Seek forgiveness for all the sins we have committed. *Inshā'Allāh* He (s.w.t.) will wipe them out. On the other hand, for the good deeds that we have, be grateful to Allah for letting us have them and try to do more.

One good deed can make a difference, no matter how small it is. And so, it is very important to also learn to be charitable. Why? Because we do not want to be from among those who want to go back to the *dunya* just to do a quick round of charity. Why would there be people who want to do this? Because the reward of being charitable for the sake of Allah is tremendous. Do not underestimate the power of a small deed that we can do, or a little statement that we can utter.

For instance, uttering the word "*SubḥānAllāh.*" This term of glorifying Allah is so powerful when put on the *Mizan*—on the scale for weighing deeds. It would be able to tip the scale. We might just need one more "*SubḥānAllāh*" to tip the scale for us to be eligible to enter *Jannah*. If we do not have it, it will be our loss. Therefore, we should keep our tongues moist with the remembrance of Allah even while reading this book. While reading this book, we can say and utter the words, "*SubḥānAllāh, Alḥamdulillāh, Mashā'Allāh, Allāhu Akbar,*" and more. We are more than capable of uttering these words and we ourselves know this as well. And so, move our tongues, and utter those words so that our tongues can bear witness that we are remembering Allah often.

In essence, obey Allah, do a lot of good deeds and seek His (s.w.t.) forgiveness for all the sins we have committed. *Inshā'Allāh*, we will be forgiven and be granted His (s.w.t.) mercy to enter *Jannah*.

Indeed, those who have **believed** and done **righteous deeds**, their Lord will **guide** them because of their **faith**. Beneath them rivers will flow in the Gardens of Pleasure.

CHAPTER 12

The Deed of Patience

Dear brothers and sisters, take with us good deeds that we can present to Allah on the Day of Judgement. I touched upon this matter in the previous chapter as well:

$$\text{يَٰٓأَيُّهَا ٱلَّذِينَ ءَامَنُوا۟ ٱتَّقُوا۟ ٱللَّهَ وَلْتَنظُرْ نَفْسٌ مَّا قَدَّمَتْ لِغَدٍ ۖ وَٱتَّقُوا۟ ٱللَّهَ ۚ إِنَّ ٱللَّهَ خَبِيرٌۢ بِمَا تَعْمَلُونَ ﴿١٨﴾}$$

O' you who have believed, fear Allah. And let every soul look to what it has put forth for tomorrow—and fear Allah. Indeed, Allah is Aware of what you do.

(Qur'an, al-Ḥashr, 59:18)

Each one of us should look at what we will present on the Day of Judgement. Perhaps it might be some of the struggles that we faced and the patience we bore through our hardships. The patience and endurance for Allah. We kept going even though it was difficult; we kept thanking Allah for granting us patience. Allah looks forward to those worshippers whom He threw so many curveballs but they remained patient through them. There are so many different challenges we go through. Some people have been struggling with their health since they were young.

Do you reckon that Allah is not watching? What do you think the struggles are designed for by Allah if not for our *Jannah*?

Do you not think that Allah has designed the struggles for us to earn *Jannah*? If you do not think that, then what do you think they are for? If we are believers, we will sail straight through all the challenges because we know that this is how we earn *Jannah*.

I recently met someone who said to make *du'a'* for them to get married soon. The person was actually wondering if marriage was something that was for them as they had already hit forty. They were unsure if they truly wanted to get married or not. And so, I told them, "If Allah has written it for you then *alḥamdulillāh*. Keep a lookout and *inshā'Allāh* if you find a decent person, you can get into it and get married. But if you don't, it is okay as well. Perhaps Allah has written something else for you. Maybe Allah has chosen you for something way beyond your imagination. And for that too, keep a lookout. Maybe Allah has chosen you to serve someone or some people; for instance a group of orphans, or a charitable work or whatever else. Perhaps, had you been married, you would not have been able to do that. Maybe. I do not know everything. Only Allah knows."

No matter the outcome of our concerns and challenges, do not be depressed. Ultimately, even if we have nothing in this world, we will have everything in *Jannah* for an eternity.

Additionally, do remember that Allah (s.w.t.) has given us a lot. He (s.w.t.) has blessed us with countless blessings. However, there are also things that perhaps He (s.w.t.) has not given us and He is testing us with it. Some people have been tested more than others and those who bear patience are the ones whom Allah is looking forward to meeting. That is why Allah (s.w.t.) says in the Qur'an:

The Ultimate Path to *Jannah*

$$\text{قُلْ يَٰعِبَادِ ٱلَّذِينَ ءَامَنُوا۟ ٱتَّقُوا۟ رَبَّكُمْ ۚ لِلَّذِينَ أَحْسَنُوا۟ فِى هَٰذِهِ ٱلدُّنْيَا حَسَنَةٌ ۗ وَأَرْضُ ٱللَّهِ وَٰسِعَةٌ ۗ إِنَّمَا يُوَفَّى ٱلصَّٰبِرُونَ أَجْرَهُم بِغَيْرِ حِسَابٍ ﴿١٠﴾}$$

Say, "O' My servants who have believed, fear your Lord. For those who do good in this world is good, and the earth of Allah is spacious. Indeed, the patient will be given their reward without account [i.e., limit]."

(Qur'an, az-Zumar, 39:10)

Those who bear patience will be given the recompense for their patience; and unlimited recompense. Despite all the struggles that we have endured, even though it almost broke us twenty or thirty times, we still push through because we love Allah; for that Allah will give us whatever we want. Whatever we ask for, Allah will give it to us. *SubḥānAllāh*. Is this worth it, dear brothers and sisters? *Wallāhi* most definitely, it is worth it.

This *dunya* is just temporary. And so, do not let it deceive us. We might have a few more days left if we are lucky and some might just have a few hours left. However, the best among us is the one who dies in a condition and state where Allah is pleased with us; meaning we die as a righteous believer.

When we die is irrelevant.

How we die is irrelevant.

However, the condition we die upon is of relevance—whether we die in the pleasure of Allah or in the displeasure of Allah.

May Allah be pleased with us. May Allah take us away when we are in a state of *iman*. May Allah grant us and allow us the ability to say the *shahadah* when we are dying. Why is this vital, brothers and sisters—to utter the *shahadah*?

It is mentioned in the following hadith that:

> The Messenger of Allah (s.a.w.) said, "He whose last words are: '*Lā ʾilāha ʾillā-llāh* (There is no true god except Allah)' will enter *Jannah*."

(Riyaḍ aṣ-Ṣaliḥin 917)

Whoever's last statement at the brink of death is, "*Lā ĭlāha ĭllā-llāh,*" shall be granted entry to *Jannah*. May Allah grant us and allow us the ability to say the *shahadah* when we are dying. *Āmīn.*

The greatest **reward** comes with the greatest **trial**.

When Allah loves someone He **tests** them.

Whoever accepts that wins His **pleasure**,

but whoever is discontent with that earns His **wrath**.

CHAPTER 13

The Meeting with the Angel of Death

A day will come when we will leave this *dunya*, *inshā'Allāh* covered in the shroud. The soul will inevitably go one day.

When the soul is leaving, a unique occurrence will happen, which is the angel will come to take the soul. Who is this angel? It is 'Izra'il, the *mala'ikah* of *maut*—the angel of death. He will come at the place and at the time that is destined for the soul to leave and nothing will change that:

$$\text{يَغْفِرْ لَكُم مِّن ذُنُوبِكُمْ وَيُؤَخِّرْكُمْ إِلَىٰ أَجَلٍ مُّسَمًّى ۚ إِنَّ أَجَلَ ٱللَّهِ إِذَا جَاءَ لَا يُؤَخَّرُ ۖ لَوْ كُنتُمْ تَعْلَمُونَ ﴿٤﴾}$$

He [i.e., Allah] will forgive you of your sins and delay you for a specified term. Indeed, the time [set by] Allah, when it comes, will not be delayed, if you only knew."

(Qur'an, Nuḥ, 71:4)

When the prescribed time of Allah comes, it will happen and it will not be delayed:

$$\text{وَلَوْ يُؤَاخِذُ ٱللَّهُ ٱلنَّاسَ بِظُلْمِهِم مَّا تَرَكَ عَلَيْهَا مِن دَابَّةٍ وَلَـٰكِن يُؤَخِّرُهُمْ إِلَىٰ أَجَلٍ مُّسَمًّى ۖ فَإِذَا جَاءَ أَجَلُهُمْ لَا يَسْتَـْٔخِرُونَ سَاعَةً ۖ وَلَا يَسْتَقْدِمُونَ ﴿٦١﴾}$$

> And if Allah were to impose blame on the people for their wrongdoing, He would not have left upon it [i.e., the earth] any creature, but He defers them for a specified term. And when their term has come, they will not remain behind an hour, nor will they precede [it].
>
> (Qur'an, an-Naḥl, 16:61)

When their fixed time comes—the appointed time of Allah—it will not be delayed by a moment or brought forward by a moment. That is Allah's time. The angel will come at that exact time to take the soul. It is mentioned in a hadith narrated by Al-Bara' ibn 'Azib, that the Prophet (s.a.w.) described the moment of departure between the souls of the righteous believers and the sinners is different.

The Righteous Believers

In the hadith by Al-Bara' ibn 'Azib, the Prophet (s.a.w.) mentioned that the angels will appear in beautiful clothing when they are taking the souls of the believers. At the same time, the angels will also give the believers assurance, by mentioning that they have done well. For the believers, when death comes, they will be happy—they will be smiling. The death of the believers will be easy and quick *inshā'Allāh*.

When the angels are about to take their souls, the angels will reassure the believers that they will be *inshā'Allāh* going to an amazing place. Furthermore, when the soul of the righteous believer is being carried away, the other angels that are passing by will ask, "Whose beautiful soul is this?" The angel will then say, "It is the soul of so-and-so."

SubḥānAllāh. Imagine our names, dear brothers and sisters, being uttered. It is also mentioned in the Qur'an that these people—the righteous believers—will be given glad tidings prior to their souls being taken away. They will be told, "Don't worry. Don't be afraid. You're going to a good place. You're going to *Jannah*," and the soul will come out of the body with ease:

$$\text{إِنَّ ٱلَّذِينَ قَالُوا۟ رَبُّنَا ٱللَّهُ ثُمَّ ٱسْتَقَـٰمُوا۟ تَتَنَزَّلُ عَلَيْهِمُ ٱلْمَلَـٰٓئِكَةُ أَلَّا تَخَافُوا۟ وَلَا تَحْزَنُوا۟ وَأَبْشِرُوا۟ بِٱلْجَنَّةِ ٱلَّتِى كُنتُمْ تُوعَدُونَ ۝}$$

Indeed, those who have said, "Our Lord is Allah" and then remained on a right course—the angels will descend upon them, [saying], "Do not fear and do not grieve but receive good tidings of Paradise, which you were promised."

(Qur'an, Fuṣṣilat, 41:30)

Those who have said, "My Lord is Allah," and remained steadfast on the path of Allah—they worshipped Allah alone, they respected and were kind to all the creatures of Allah—will be told by the angels during the time of their death, "Do not fear and do not be sad. You have no reason to be in fear or in sadness because glad tidings have been promised for you. *Jannah* is waiting for you."

SubḥānAllāh. Imagine this, brothers and sisters, the angels telling us, "We are taking you to *Jannah*. You are going to *Jannah*." How wonderful is this!

Al-Bara' ibn 'Azib said:

We went out with the Prophet to the funeral of a man of the Anṣar and came to the grave. It had not yet been dug, so God's messenger sat down and we sat down around him quietly. He had in his hand a stick with which he was making marks on the ground. Then he raised his head and said, "Seek refuge in God from the punishment of the grave saying it twice or thrice." He then said, "When a believer is about to leave the world and go forward to the next world, angels with faces white as the sun come down to him from heaven with one of the shrouds of Paradise and some of the perfume of Paradise and sit away from him as far as the eye can see. Then the angel of death comes and sits at his head and says, 'Good soul, come out to forgiveness and acceptance from God.' It then comes out as a drop flows from a water-skin and he seizes it; and when he does so, they do not leave it in his hand for an instant, but take it and place it in that shroud and that perfume, and from it there comes forth a fragrance like that of the sweetest musk found on the face of the earth.

The Ultimate Path to *Jannah*

They then take it up and do not bring it past a company of angels without their asking, 'Who is this good soul?' to which they reply, 'So and so, the son of so and so,' using the best of his names by which people called him on the earth. They then bring him to the lowest heaven and ask that the gate should be opened for him. This is done, and from every heaven its archangels escort him to the next heaven until he is brought to the seventh heaven, and God who is great and glorious says, 'Record the book of my servant in *Illiyyun* (Cf. Qur'an, al-Muṭaffifin, 83:18) and take him back to earth, for I created mankind from it, I shall return them into it, and from it I shall bring them forth another time.' His soul is then restored to his body, two angels come to him, and making him sit up say to him, 'Who is your Lord?' He replies, 'My Lord is God.' They ask, 'What is your religion?' and he replies, 'My religion is Islam.' They ask, 'Who is this man who was sent among you?' and he replies, 'He is God's messenger.' They ask, 'What is your [source of] knowledge?' and he replies, 'I have read God's Book, believed in it and declared it to be true.' Then one cries from heaven, 'My servant has spoken the truth, so spread out carpets from Paradise for him, clothe him from Paradise, and open a gate for him into Paradise.' Then some of its joy and fragrance comes to him, his grave is made spacious for him as far as the eye can see, and a man with a beautiful face, beautiful garments and a sweet odour comes to him and says, 'Rejoice in what pleases you for this is your day which you have been promised.' He asks, 'Who are you, for your face is perfectly beautiful and brings good?' He replies, 'I am your good deeds.' He then says, 'My Lord, bring the last hour; my Lord, bring the last hour, so that I may return to my people and my property…'

(Mishkat al-Maṣabiḥ 1630)

The Sinners

In the latter part of the hadith by Al-Bara' ibn 'Azib, the departure of the souls of the sinners is also described.

The people who indulged in sins, the people who were never connected to Allah (s.w.t.), the people who disobeyed Allah's commands, the people who worshipped other than Allah—they will have their souls taken away in an excruciating manner. Their souls will be taken in a very tough and painful way.

Imagine this: A rope which has spikes on it being pulled out of the throat. May Allah the Almighty protect us.

Al-Bara' ibn 'Azib said:

> ...But when an infidel is about to leave the world and proceed to the next world, angels with black faces come down to him from heaven with hair-cloth and sit away from him as far as the eye can see. Then the angel of death comes and sits at his head and says, 'Wicked soul, come out to displeasure from God.' Then it becomes dissipated in his body, and he draws it out as a spit is drawn out from

moistened wool. He then seizes it, and when he does so they do not leave it in his hand for an instant, but put it in that hair-cloth and from it there comes forth a stench like the most offensive stench of a corpse found on the face of the earth. They then take it up and do not bring it past a company of angels without their asking, 'Who is this wicked soul?' to which they reply, 'So and so, the son of so and so,' using the worst names he was called in the world. When he is brought to the lowest heaven, request is made that the gate be opened for him, but it is not opened for him." God's Messenger then recited, "The gates of heaven will not be opened for them and they will not enter Paradise until a camel can pass through the eye of a needle (Qur'an, al-A'raf, 7:40). God who is Great and Glorious then says, 'Record his book in *Sijjin* (Cf. Qur'an, al-Mutaffifin, 83:7) in the lowest earth,' and his soul is thrown down.'" He then recited, "He who assigns partners to God is as if he had fallen down from heaven and been snatched up by birds, or made to fall by the wind in a place far distant (Qur'an, al-Hajj, 22:31). His soul is then restored to his body, two angels come to him, and making him sit up say to him, 'Who is your Lord?' He replies, 'Alas, alas, I do not know.' They ask, 'What is your religion?' and he replies, 'Alas, alas, I do not know.' They ask, 'Who is this man who was sent among you?' and he replies, 'Alas, alas, I do not know.' Then one cries from heaven, 'He has lied, so spread out carpets from hell for him, and open a gate for him into hell.' Then some of its heat and hot air comes to him, his grave is made narrow for him so that his ribs are pressed together in it, and a man with an ugly face, ugly garments and an offensive odour comes to him and says, 'Be grieved with what displeases you, for this is your day which you have been promised.' He asks, 'Who are you, for your face is most ugly and brings evil?' He replies, 'I am your wicked deeds.' He then says, 'My Lord, do not bring the last hour.'" In a version, there is something similar containing an addition: "When his soul comes out, every angel between heaven and earth and every angel in heaven invokes blessings on him, and the gates of heaven are opened for him, no guardians of a gate failing to supplicate God that his soul may be taken up beyond them. But his soul, i.e., the infidel's, is pulled out along with the veins and every angel between heaven and earth and every angel in heaven curses him, and the gates of heaven are locked, no guardians of a gate failing to supplicate God that his soul may not be taken up beyond them."

(Mishkat al-Maṣabiḥ 1630)

The description of when the souls of the sinners are taken is very vivid in the above hadith. They will be struggling and suffering when their souls are taken. This is how it will be for the wicked people—the ones who were evil, the ones who committed mass murder, the ones who wanted to do whatever they wanted to do and were far away from the *deen* of Allah. Among them are the ones who thought there were other Gods besides Allah the Almighty and the ones who uttered they believed in Allah but in truth their hearts did not believe.

To these people, Allah the Almighty gives them time before the Ultimate day comes. Why does Allah give them time? Because perhaps they might turn and repent. In surah an-Naḥl which I mentioned in the early part of this chapter, Allah says, *"And if Allah were to impose blame on the people for their wrongdoing, He would not have left upon it [i.e., the earth] any creature, but He defers them for a specified term."*

Allah the Almighty is forbearing and merciful. He gives time so that they may repent. There are also people who are given time to realise that the reason for their punishment is due to their actions. And so, Allah does things for His own reasoning.

Every soul will taste death.

And We test you with evil and with good as trial,

and to Us you will be returned.

CHAPTER 14

The Realm After Death

Let us delve into how long the souls will feel the Day of Judgement is away.

To some souls, the Day of Judgement will be near but to some, it will be very far. For the righteous believers, for the ones who die as good souls—the distance between the time of death and the Day of Judgement will pass in a flash. The good souls will feel that they only rested for a day or part of a day, *SubḥānAllāh*. And the Day of Judgement for them, will also be completed fast:

Abu Hurayrah reported:

The Prophet (s.a.w.) said, "The Day of Resurrection for the believers will be like the length of time between noon and afternoon prayers."

(al-Firdaws lil-Daylami 8893)

On the contrary, the disbelievers, the souls of the people who were evil—the distance between the time of death and the Day of Judgement will pass slowly. Time is prolonged for them and it will feel like they have to wait for fifty thousand years:

سَأَلَ سَآئِلٌۢ بِعَذَابٍ وَاقِعٍ ۝ لِّلْكَٰفِرِينَ لَيْسَ لَهُۥ دَافِعٌ ۝ مِّنَ ٱللَّهِ ذِى ٱلْمَعَارِجِ ۝ تَعْرُجُ ٱلْمَلَٰٓئِكَةُ وَٱلرُّوحُ إِلَيْهِ فِى يَوْمٍ كَانَ مِقْدَارُهُۥ خَمْسِينَ أَلْفَ سَنَةٍ ۝

A supplicant asked for a punishment bound to happen to the disbelievers; of it there is no preventer. [It is] from Allah, Owner of the ways of ascent. The angels and the Spirit [i.e.,

> Jibril] will ascend to Him during a Day the extent of which is fifty thousand years.
>
> (Qur'an, al-Ma'arij, 70:1-4)

It is similar to that of a prisoner on a death sentence. When someone is on the death sentence, time is moving excruciatingly slowly for them as they await their execution and punishment. They cannot sleep and are always restless. It is as if time does not move for them at all. Why? Because they are waiting for something bad. Even on the Day of Judgement, it will not be easy for them. It will be a very difficult day for them.

The grave will either be a garden from the gardens of Paradise,

or a pit from the pits of the Fire.

CHAPTER 15

Friends and Foes

In Chapter 13, I touched upon the sinners, those who are evil and that some are given time by Allah so that they may repent.

I would like for you, dear readers, to imagine this situation: Someone does something wrong to us and we pray to Allah to take them away. We pray and say to Allah, "O' Allah, take them away," because we are hurt and in so much pain because of them.

This is a situation that we are all familiar with. We have seen this around us. I once heard a man saying, "Oh so-and-so claims that the angel came to him. I hope it's the angel of death." This man was hoping that the person would die. This happens to us. Sometimes, people hurt us so much that we just want

Allah to take them away. However, the thing is Allah gives some of these people time for a reason.

Imagine this: Allah gives the people who hurt us time and life. In a few years, their hard hearts soften up and they change and become a better person. They then come to us and apologise. We then become close friends—best friends.

Do you think this scenario is possible? Yes, and only by the will of Allah:

> ۞ عَسَى ٱللَّهُ أَن يَجْعَلَ بَيْنَكُمْ وَبَيْنَ ٱلَّذِينَ عَادَيْتُم مِّنْهُم مَّوَدَّةً ۚ وَٱللَّهُ قَدِيرٌ ۚ وَٱللَّهُ غَفُورٌ رَّحِيمٌ ۝

Perhaps Allah will put, between you and those to whom you have been enemies among them, affection. And Allah is competent, and Allah is Forgiving and Merciful.

(Qur'an, al-Mumtaḥanah, 60:7)

Allah is able and more than capable of creating love between us and our enemies. It is possible that the person we hate and dislike will one day become someone who is precious to us—someone who we will love dearly. It is just a matter of time. It can happen and it has happened. It also happened at the time of the Prophet Muḥammad (s.a.w.). It has also happened in our own lives but not always.

Sometimes it does not happen because that is what Allah has written for us. Sometimes our enemies remain as our enemies or they might become worse enemies as time passes by. Only Allah alone knows.

In essence, when the person is evil, their days are numbered. Allah gives them time to repent. And if they do not, it is to prove to them on the Day of Judgement the consequences of their actions. They were given time to turn back to the ultimate path of Allah but they did not.

Do not **hate** one another, and do not be **jealous** of one another, and do not **desert** each other. Always remain **brothers** unto each other.

CHAPTER 16

Good Company

We must not lose our focus on *Jannah*. The only thing that we need to constantly remember is to prepare for the Hereafter so that we will go to the right place.

Let me give an example. Imagine driving in Putrajaya or Kuala Lumpur and missing a turn. When that happens, we would be worried about our fuel and will go to the nearest petrol station to fill it up. The question is, why are we worried? Because we missed a turn. Therefore, we must read the navigation properly so that we do not miss the turn.

The same with *Jannah*. We must read the navigation to *Jannah* properly. We must read the map to *Jannah* properly so that we do not miss a turn and end up at a place we do not want to be. If we miss a turn, it might lead us to a place we do not want to be at or we might go somewhere else before we get to our destination. We all want to go straight to *Jannah*. None of us would want to go to *Jannah* via *Jahannam*. So be careful. May Allah forgive us and grant us protection.

Additionally, imagine if we took a bad turn and ended up with a flat tyre. At the same time, the fuel ran out and we were stranded under the scorching sun. We ended up in that situation because we took a bad turn. Furthermore, if we had company with us, they would be furious as well. They will be angry because our bad turn affected them as well. Some people will even hold a grudge on these kinds of incidents for years. Therefore, pay heed to the people we keep around us, dear brothers and sisters.

Yes, we made a human error. And so, we must fix it and get back on the road to our destination. We must seek forgiveness and repent. With our company, seek forgiveness as well for the mistakes we have made. However, sometimes even after we have apologised for our errors, there will be people who will hold grudges against us for a long time. They will still blame us for being stranded in Kuala Lumpur even though it happened five years ago. And so, these are the companies we have to be wary of.

We have to make sure we have good company—people who will remind us not to take bad turns, people who will guide us to the right destination.

When we are reading the map to *Jannah*, we must have people around us who will remind us and say, "Be careful. Don't turn here. Remember to go straight ahead," or "Hey, don't take the wrong turn. I know others who have been here. So be careful."

Let me give an example in regard to *ṣalah*. When we are with good people, they will tell us, "Hey, let's pray." Even though there are still ten more minutes before the *Maghrib* prayer, they will tell us to start planning and preparing early for the prayer. There are people like this, aren't there? Those people are the good ones, so keep them close. With them around, we would not miss our turn and would go straight to our destination *inshā'Allāh*.

Overall, it is very important to have good friends and people in our circle.

The Prophet (s.a.w.) mentioned in a hadith that we will be resurrected with the people we love:

'Ali reported:

The Messenger of Allah (s.a.w.), said, "... No man loves a people except that he will be resurrected with them."

(al-Muʻjam al-Awsaṭ 6450)

Ponder about this, dear brothers and sisters: Who do we love? Who do we want to be resurrected with? Do we have good company around us who we want to be resurrected with? Do we love the right people? Or do we love the wrong people?

If we love the wrong people—the ones who indulge in sin and are not firm on the *deen* of Allah, where do we think we will be resurrected? It will be in *Jahannam*. Do we really want to be resurrected with the wrong people then? No. We all want to be with the good people, with *aṣ-Ṣadiqin*—the truthful ones, the prophets, the ones who are loved by Allah and those who love Allah. Therefore, be among those people who love the right people and *inshāʾAllāh* we will be resurrected with those good company in the Hereafter:

Narrated Anas (r.a.):

A man asked the Prophet (s.a.w.) about the Hour (i.e. Day of Judgement), saying, "When will the Hour be?" The Prophet (s.a.w.) said, "What have you prepared for it?" The man said, "Nothing, except that I love Allah and His Apostle." The Prophet (s.a.w.) said, "You will be with those whom you love." We had never been so glad as we were on hearing that saying of the Prophet (i.e., "You will be with those whom you love.") Therefore, I love the Prophet, Abu Bakr and 'Umar, and I hope that I will be with them because of my love for them though my deeds are not similar to theirs.

(Ṣaḥīḥ al-Bukhari 3688)

In essence, a good company will help us retain our focus on the path to *Jannah*.

The similitude of **good company** and that of **bad company**

is that of the owner of musk and of the one blowing the bellows.

The **owner** of musk would either offer you some **perfume** as a present,

or you would buy it from him,

or you will get a **good fragrance** from him.

As for the one who blows the bellows—the **blacksmith**,

he either burns your clothes,

or you will get a repugnant and **bad fragrance** from him.

PART 3

The Essence of *Jannah*

CHAPTER 17

The Gates of *Jannah* and *Jahannam*

In the Qur'an, the manner of the people of *Jannah* and *Jahannam* entering their destinations is described. Those who were conscious of Allah and developed the correct relationship with Him will be driven to Paradise in groups:

وَسِيقَ ٱلَّذِينَ ٱتَّقَوْا۟ رَبَّهُمْ إِلَى ٱلْجَنَّةِ زُمَرًا ۖ حَتَّىٰٓ إِذَا جَآءُوهَا وَفُتِحَتْ أَبْوَٰبُهَا وَقَالَ لَهُمْ خَزَنَتُهَا سَلَـٰمٌ عَلَيْكُمْ طِبْتُمْ فَٱدْخُلُوهَا خَـٰلِدِينَ ﴿٧٣﴾

> But those who feared their Lord will be driven to Paradise in groups until, when they reach it while its gates have been opened and its keepers say, "Peace be upon you; you have become pure; so enter it to abide eternally therein," [they will enter].

(Qur'an, az-Zumar, 39:73)

What happens to the people of *Jannah* as they are walking to the eternal abode of bliss? The gates of *Jannah* will be wide open for them.

Let me give an example to explain this. In the *dunya*, when the VIPs are walking around, the door will be opened for them before they even enter the place. When they get to the door, it is already wide open for them, and they just have to enter it. They just have to keep moving. Why? Because they are the VIPs. No one stops them. The same goes for the dwellers of *Jannah*. They are the VIPs of *Jannah*.

That is why in the above verse of surah az-Zumar, Allah describes and says, "*When they reach it while its gates have been opened and its keepers say, 'Peace be upon you; you have become pure; so enter it to abide eternally therein,' [they will enter]*."

When the people of Paradise get to the doors of Paradise, they will find them wide open. They will be greeted by the gatekeepers of Paradise and will enter *Jannah*. The gatekeepers of *Jannah* will mention to them, "Peace be upon you. You have done really well. And so, now you may enter this place and abide here forever."

On the other hand, in verse 71 and 72 of surah az-Zumar, Allah describes the people of hell entering *Jahannam*:

وَسِيقَ ٱلَّذِينَ كَفَرُوٓاْ إِلَىٰ جَهَنَّمَ زُمَرًا حَتَّىٰٓ إِذَا جَآءُوهَا فُتِحَتْ أَبْوَٰبُهَا وَقَالَ لَهُمْ خَزَنَتُهَآ أَلَمْ يَأْتِكُمْ رُسُلٌ مِّنكُمْ يَتْلُونَ عَلَيْكُمْ ءَايَٰتِ رَبِّكُمْ وَيُنذِرُونَكُمْ لِقَآءَ يَوْمِكُمْ هَٰذَا ۚ قَالُواْ بَلَىٰ وَلَٰكِنْ حَقَّتْ كَلِمَةُ ٱلْعَذَابِ عَلَى ٱلْكَٰفِرِينَ ﴿٧١﴾ قِيلَ ٱدْخُلُوٓاْ أَبْوَٰبَ جَهَنَّمَ خَٰلِدِينَ فِيهَا ۖ فَبِئْسَ مَثْوَى ٱلْمُتَكَبِّرِينَ ﴿٧٢﴾

> And those who disbelieved will be driven to Hell in groups until, when they reach it, its gates are opened and its keepers will say, "Did there not come to you messengers from yourselves, reciting to you the verses of your Lord and warning you of the meeting of this Day of yours?" They will say, "Yes, but the word [i.e., decree] of punishment has come into effect upon the disbelievers." [To them] it will be said, "Enter the gates of Hell to abide eternally therein, and wretched is the residence of the arrogant."
>
> (Qur'an, az-Zumar, 39:71-72)

The difference between these descriptions can be seen in verses 71 and 73 which is that there is a difference in just one letter—the letter و *(wau)*.

For the people of *Jannah*, the *ayah* says *wa futiḥat*—which means that the doors are already open; the doors are waiting and we are going straight into them.

However, the people of *Jahannam* will get there like criminals entering a prison. At the prison, when the criminals are walking to enter prison, the doors are not wide open. If the doors were wide open before they reached, what would happen? The other criminals will rush out. And so that is why, the doors will only be opened when they reach them. Basically, the doors are closed and they will only be opened when the people of *Jahannam* reach them.

So the و indicates the people of *Jannah*, that when they get there, the doors are opened for them and they are welcomed. The missing presence of the و in the *ayah* of the people of *Jahannam* means the doors shall only be opened when they get to them. And so we can see the difference in situation between the people of *Jahannam* and the people of *Jannah*. The people of *Jahannam* are not like the VIPs of *Jannah*. It is only for the people of *Jannah* that the carpet is laid open. Whatever it is going to be on that day, only Allah knows best.

In essence, the dwellers of *Jannah* and *Jahannam* will be treated differently. Therefore focus on the path to *Jannah*, do good deeds and look forward to the meeting with Allah.

And those who were **mindful** of their Lord will be led to Paradise in successive groups. When they arrive at its already opened gates, its keepers will say, "Peace be upon you! You have done well, so come in, to stay forever."

CHAPTER 18

The People of *Jahannam* in *Jannah*

Dear brothers and sisters, I want to touch upon the people we will *inshā'Allāh* remember in *Jannah*. I mentioned in Chapter 9 that we probably would not remember our lives in the *dunya* except that which Allah allows.

When we are *inshā'Allāh* in *Jannah*—may Allah grant us all Paradise—we will remember someone from the *dunya* and we would like to meet them. However, if it just so happens that the person is in Hellfire. What will happen then? We are in Paradise, the place where we can have and see everything that we want, but the person we want to meet with right now is not there because they are in *Jahannam*.

So, what will happen then? Will we not get to see them at all or will they be brought out of *Jahannam*? What will take place in *Jannah*? It is the latter. Allah (s.w.t.) will bring that person out of *Jahannam* and will bring them to *Jannah*. It will never be the case that if we remember someone in *Jannah*, they will remain in *Jahannam*.

Here in this *dunya*, we tend to tell people, "Please remember me when you go to *Jannah*." We say it without knowing that perhaps it might be the other way around. We do not know the hidden sins of people. May Allah forgive us all.

And so, we do not know who is going to *Jannah* first and who will go next and so on. It is easy to say and ask people to remember us in *Jannah*. However, Allah (s.w.t.) will only allow us to remember those people who He (s.w.t.) has already decided and approved will enter *Jannah*. It is not because we remember them that they will enter *Jannah*. No. It is by the will and mercy of Allah. It is by Allah's mercy that we will remember those people as Allah wants them to be in *Jannah*.

In essence, when we remember someone while we are in *Jannah*—a person who is in *Jahannam*—it is because Allah (s.w.t.) wants to take them out from the very beginning. It is not because of us who remember them that they are brought to *Jannah*. No. It is by Allah's mercy. They are put into *Jannah* because Allah knows that they deserve to be out of *Jahannam*.

Do you reckon that Allah would give someone something they do not deserve? Allah's mercy is greater than anything we can imagine. So, Allah will take them out of *Jahannam* and will bring them to *Jannah*, *subḥānAllāh*.

No one will enter *Jannah* by his deeds and actions,

but only because of Allah's Infinite Mercy.

CHAPTER 19

The One Who Loves to Meet Allah

Dear brothers and sisters, look forward to the meeting with Allah the Almighty.

Looking forward to the meeting with Allah is so powerful. No matter how sinful we may be, the fact is we are believers. We believe in our Maker and we look forward to meeting Him. And so, Allah the Almighty also looks forward to meeting with us:

It was narrated from 'A'ishah that the Messenger of Allah (s.a.w.) said:

> "Whoever loves to meet Allah, Allah loves to meet him, and whoever hates to meet Allah, Allah hates to meet him." It was said to him: "O' Messenger of Allah, does hating to meet Allah mean hating to meet death? For all of us hate death." He said: "No. Rather that is only at the moment of death. But if he is given the glad tidings of the mercy and forgiveness of Allah, he loves to meet Allah and Allah loves to meet him; and if he is given the tidings of the punishment of Allah, he hates to meet Allah and Allah hates to meet him."

(Sunan ibn Majah 4264)

Whoever looks forward to the meeting with Allah, Allah looks forward to meeting him. The term "*aḥabba*" means "loves" and this is the expression used in the hadith above—"Whoever loves to meet Allah, Allah loves to meet him." *SubḥānAllāh*. Imagine Allah looking forward to meeting us just because we are looking forward to meeting Him (s.w.t.).

Meeting Allah is just on a whole other level. In the *dunya*, when we are looking forward to meeting someone, the reason will be because they are famous.

It is due to their fame, their celebrity status and their TikTok posts.

What do you think is the reason for Allah wanting to meet us? Because we prayed to Him (s.w.t.), we called out to Him (s.w.t.), we cried to Him (s.w.t.), we fasted for Him (s.w.t.), we went to *hajj* for Him (s.w.t.), we were charitable for Him (s.w.t.), we stopped ourselves from doing certain things for Him (s.w.t.); we did things for Him (s.w.t.).

Allah looks forward to meeting us because we went through all the challenges He gave us with *ṣabr*. Some of us lost our children, parents and loved ones, some of us went through a divorce, some of us lost our jobs and more, but we bore patience and we cried to Him (s.w.t.). Every single time we went through challenges and difficulties, we kept saying *'Innallāha ma'aṣ-ṣābirīn*—Surely Allah is with those who are patient:

$$... إِنَّ ٱللَّهَ مَعَ ٱلصَّٰبِرِينَ ...$$

...Indeed, Allah is with the patient.

(Qur'an, al-Baqarah, 2:153)

Therefore, dear brothers and sisters, know this: The challenges in this world are nothing compared to the beauty of the day we will be meeting Allah (s.w.t.). Whenever we are going through something, tell ourselves, "A day will come when I will meet Allah the Almighty and He (s.w.t.) will grant me *Jannah*."

Look at what is happening to Palestine, dear brothers and sisters. We feel so helpless because we are not the powerful ones who have the means to help them. We only have the means to help them to a certain degree and that is making lots of *du'a'* for them, humanitarian assistance, creating awareness and so on. Besides that, what do we have? We only have Allah and we have no one besides Allah.

Do not expect anything from anyone except Allah (s.w.t.). No matter what challenges we are going through, the Palestinians are going through more. What is the worst thing that could happen to them and the best thing that could happen to them? These two things are almost similar in the eyes of the believers. According to this world, the worst thing that could happen is that they are martyred.

If they are martyred, they will go back to Allah (s.w.t.) and they will go to *Jannah*. Allah will look forward to meeting them because despite the immense struggle, they chose to be patient for the sake of Allah, they chose to be steadfast on the path of Allah. Therefore, Allah looks forward to meeting them.

Isn't that wonderful? Isn't meeting Allah the best thing ever? That is why Allah gives the martyrs one of the highest ranks. So for them, it is a victory. That is why when we see the Palestinians, they are saying, "My brother was martyred, *alhamdulillāh*," "My sister was martyred, *alhamdulillāh*," and, "My husband was martyred, *alhamdulillāh*." It is crazy. The whole world looks at them and wonders how they are so calm.

Why are they calm? Because they are believers. The believer is always calm. What is the ultimate worst thing that can happen from a worldly perspective? We lose our lives. What is the best thing that can happen? We enter *Jannah*. In order to enter *Jannah*, we will first have to come out of this life.

فَٱسْتَجَابَ لَهُمْ رَبُّهُمْ أَنِّى لَآ أُضِيعُ عَمَلَ عَٰمِلٍ مِّنكُم مِّن ذَكَرٍ أَوْ أُنثَىٰ ۖ بَعْضُكُم مِّنۢ بَعْضٍ ۖ فَٱلَّذِينَ هَاجَرُوا۟

The Ultimate Path to *Jannah*

وَأُخْرِجُواْ مِن دِيَـٰرِهِمْ وَأُوذُواْ فِى سَبِيلِى وَقَـٰتَلُواْ وَقُتِلُواْ لَأُكَفِّرَنَّ عَنْهُمْ سَيِّـَٔاتِهِمْ وَلَأُدْخِلَنَّهُمْ جَنَّـٰتٍ تَجْرِى مِن تَحْتِهَا ٱلْأَنْهَـٰرُ ثَوَابًا مِّنْ عِندِ ٱللَّهِ ۗ وَٱللَّهُ عِندَهُۥ حُسْنُ ٱلثَّوَابِ ﴿١٩٥﴾

And their Lord responded to them, "Never will I allow to be lost the work of [any] worker among you, whether male or female; you are of one another. So those who emigrated or were evicted from their homes or were harmed in My cause or fought or were killed—I will surely remove from them their misdeeds, and I will surely admit them to gardens beneath which rivers flow as reward from Allah, and Allah has with Him the best reward."

(Qur'an, Ali-'Imran, 3:195)

When Allah loves a slave, He calls Jibril and says: "I love so-and-so; so love him."

Then Jibril loves him.

After that he (Jibril) announces to the **inhabitants** of **heavens** that Allah loves so-and-so; so love him;

and the inhabitants of the heavens (the **angels**) also love him,

and then make people on earth love him.

CHAPTER 20

Perfection in *Jannah*

As I mentioned in Chapter 7, we are beautiful in the way Allah has created us. However, in this chapter, I will be taking the approach in a slightly different lens.

When we say and think that someone is beautiful and handsome, the reality is we all have imperfections. Perfection is still coming. Perfection is in *Jannah*. Every one of us has a flaw or two, or more. Something might be wrong with our toes; from one foot to the other there has to be something slightly different. *Jannah* is where there will be perfection.

Allah created *Jannah* and it is there we will have perfection, not in this *dunya*. He (s.w.t.) will not give it to us here. Something has to go amiss. Our ears might be slightly different; perhaps one is bigger and the other is straighter. Some might say, "But I look like Mickey Mouse." It is okay. Some people like Mickey Mouse so it is fine. There is nothing wrong with that. That is the way Allah has made us. In Allah's eyes, our imperfection is beautiful. He made us all in the best of form. *Mashā'Allāh*. Be happy.

If there is something we feel is wrong with ourselves—meaning an abnormality in our features that affects our health—we are permitted to undergo a procedure to correct it. If it is disrupting our health, we can undergo surgery to correct it. However, undergoing a procedure just for the purpose of trying it out, for fun, or just because we do not like our features, is not good. This matter is not something to be played with.

I know a few people who are suicidal because they had surgery to fix something that they just did not like about themselves. Some went to have a nose job done when there was nothing wrong with their nose, and now they cannot stand the way they look and have health problems. Some cannot even breathe properly anymore. Some became suicidal and unfortunately committed suicide. This is the reality. There are a lot of similar incidents that have happened.

When we scroll through the web or social media, we will find this information. Why did they commit suicide? Because they changed what Allah had made for them when there was nothing wrong with it.

If there is something wrong, we are allowed to correct it and have a procedure. For instance, perhaps someone has six fingers instead of five. They are allowed to live with it and they are also allowed to have a procedure to remove the extra finger. If our nose is bothering us due to serious health issues, then we are allowed to undergo surgery. However, if there is nothing wrong with it, then let it be, leave it. It is fine as it is. If there is a slight difference in our ears, for instance, it is okay. That is normal. Some might say, "But no one will love me." No, there will be. There will be someone who only wants those ears or hands. They would probably look at us and say, "I was looking for you all my life."

In essence, Allah created perfection for the Hereafter. The day we enter *Jannah*, we will be so gorgeous, so amazing, and so beautiful just the way we want it. If we are already wowed by what we find beautiful in this *dunya*, the beauty of *Jannah* is way greater than anything; it is unimaginable. Whatever amazes us in this *dunya*, we will forget about it once we are in *Jannah* because what we will find there is more amazing. The only thing we need to remember is to prepare for that day so that we will go to the right place.

Jannah is a place where no eye has ever **seen**,

no ear has ever **heard**,

and no mind has ever **imagined**.

CHAPTER 21

Spouses in Jannah

Dear brothers and sisters, I would like to tell you something interesting about Jannah.

Inshā'Allāh we will be with our spouses in *Jannah*. However, when we look at our spouse there, they will appear in the way we want him or her to be. Meaning, their height, their size, their features, their way of talking—whatever we disliked about them will now be according to our liking.

$$\text{ٱدْخُلُوا۟ ٱلْجَنَّةَ أَنتُمْ وَأَزْوَٰجُكُمْ تُحْبَرُونَ ۝}$$

Enter Paradise, you and your kinds, delighted.

(Qur'an, az-Zukhruf, 43:70)

And so, our husband or wife will appear in a way that delights us. However, our spouses will also be in *Jannah* the way they want to be. And so, there might be a small clash here. Perhaps the husband wants to be tall, handsome, and muscular with black hair and black eyes. However, the wife wants him to appear perhaps slightly shorter with blonde hair and blue eyes.

What do you think will happen if there is this clash?

In *Jannah*, each of the spouses will look exactly how they want to be. This means that when the husband is looking at himself, he is the way he wants himself to be. And when the wife looks at him, he appears in the way she wants him to be. *SubḥānAllāh*, it is mind-boggling. How is this possible? I do not know, dear brothers and sisters. This is Allah. We do not know how Allah the Almighty does it. However, what we do know is that Allah said in the Qur'an:

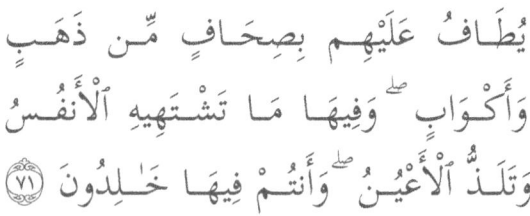

> Circulated among them will be plates and vessels of gold. And therein is whatever the souls desire and [what] delights the eyes, and you will abide therein eternally.
>
> (Qur'an, az-Zukhruf, 43:71)

In *Jannah*, there will be that which is tasty to the eyes, that which is sweet to the eyes. Whatever is there will delight the eyes and we will have whatever the soul desires. I mentioned as well in the previous chapter that *Jannah* is a place that surpasses all imaginations:

Narrated Abu Hurayrah:

> The Prophet (s.a.w.) said, "Allah said, 'I have prepared for My pious worshippers such things as no eye has ever seen, no ear has ever heard of, and nobody has ever thought of. All that is reserved, besides which, all that you have seen, is nothing.'" Then he recited: "No soul knows what is kept hidden (in reserve) for them of joy as a reward for what they used to do (Qur'an, as-Sajdah, 32:17)."
>
> (Ṣaḥīḥ al-Bukhari 4780)

In the above hadith, Allah the Almighty says that He has prepared for His pious servants, that which no eye has seen, no ear has heard and that which has never crossed any mind or heart. *SubḥānAllāh*. That is what has been prepared. Therefore, the goal is to just get there—to the eternal abode of bliss. Just imagine how beautiful and perfect we will be in *Jannah*.

How will we recognise the people there in *Jannah*? We will recognise them in the way Allah wants us to recognise them. There might be cases where perhaps the spouse we had in the *dunya* might not make it into *Jannah*.

What do you think will happen then? I do not know but what I do know is that Allah will never let us down.

Remember this always: Allah will never let us down.

Whatever it is, whether it is about our spouse or our pets being in *Jannah* or not, at this moment we do not know. As I mentioned earlier, if we want to know whether they are there or not, get there first. Get onto the ultimate path and reach the final destination—*Jannah*. When we are there, we will have whatever we wish and desire:

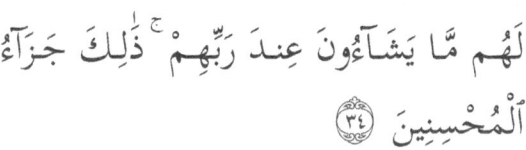

They will have whatever they desire with their Lord. That is the reward of the doers of good.

(Qur'an, az-Zumar, 39:34)

Allah will never let us down. Thus, focus on getting there instead of focusing too much on what is there and what is not there.

When a **husband** and **wife** look at each other with **love**, **Allah** looks at both with **Mercy**.

CHAPTER 22

The Wish List That Will Not Exist

Dear brothers and sisters, I mentioned that, *inshā'Allāh*, when we get to *Jannah* we will have whatever we wish for. I also mentioned that we should focus on getting to *Jannah* instead of thinking about what we will and will not have there.

If we were to write up a wish list of all the things that we want in *Jannah*, then we are fools. We would all be fools to do that. Why? Because we are going to write up a wish list of things that will not exist.

Let me give an example: If we were in the womb of our mother and we wanted to write up a wish list for what we want when we get to Earth, what would we write? We do not even know what is on the other side. The fluids and nutrients we were surrounded by in the womb, would we want that today? No. If I were to offer any of us what we enjoyed in the womb here on this Earth, the reaction would be, "Eww. No!"

Why would we have that reaction? We enjoyed it and we were nurtured in the womb for nine months due to it. We were protected in the womb of our mother but there is nothing that we remember from there.

Furthermore, just as how we forget about our life in the womb of our mother, we might not remember much about life in this *dunya*. We will only remember certain things. Allah will let us remember certain things for purposes that only He knows best. However, when it comes to the main things that we want and wish for, we will not remember them. That is why the best thing to wish and make *du'a'* for is *Jannah*.

Ask and supplicate to Allah to want to enter *Jannah*. That is enough. That *du'a'* is sufficient. Once we enter *Jannah*, we will have all the perks. Once we enter *Jannah*, we can decide what we want. *SubḥānAllāh*. May Allah take us all to enter *Jannah*:

لَهُم مَّا يَشَآءُونَ فِيهَا وَلَدَيْنَا مَزِيدٌ ﴿٣٥﴾

They will have whatever they wish therein, and with Us is more.

(Qur'an, Qaf, 50:35)

The dwellers of *Jannah* will have whatever they wish for in it.

Additionally, they will have extra. What is that extra? What more would Allah want to give us? It is the meeting with Him (s.w.t.).

The **life** of this world
is no more than the
delusion of enjoyment.
Death is certain and
life is not.
But *Jannah* is
eternal.
In *Jannah*, we will have
whatever we **wish** for.
In *Jannah*, we will have
everlasting happiness.

PART 4

Supplications and Acts for the Ultimate Meeting

CHAPTER 23

Duʿaʾ for the Best Ending

Dear readers, we should always supplicate and ask Allah to allow us to make the best of our days, our last moments before we depart from this world, as well as making the best of our days the day we meet Him (s.w.t.):

اللَّهُمَّ اجْعَلْ خَيْرَ عُمْرِي آخِرَهُ، وَخَيْرَ عَمَلِي خَوَاتِمَهُ، وَاجْعَلْ خَيْرَ أَيَّامِي يَوْمَ أَلْقَاكَ

"Allāhumma-jʿal khaira ʿumrī ākhirahu, wa khaira ʿamalī khawātimahu, wa-jʿal khaira ayyāmī yauma ʾalqāka."

"O' Allah, make the best of my life be the end of it, the best of my deeds the last of them, and the best of my days the day upon which I will meet You."

('Amal al-Yawm wal-Laylah 121)

There are **no sad endings**, for those who **trust Allah.**

CHAPTER 24

Du'ā' for the Meeting with Allah

In Jannah, we will have whatever we wish for. However, the ultimate gift is the meeting with Allah. SubḥānAllāh.

Everything that has impressed us on this Earth and everything that will impress us in *Jannah* is nothing compared to the meeting with Allah the Almighty. We will be most impressed, wowed and amazed when we meet the Creator of the entire creation—the Creator of you and I—Allah the Almighty. How will that meeting be? We do not know much but look forward to it. Pray for it.

The Ultimate Path to *Jannah*

Supplicate and ask Allah (s.w.t.) to grant us the best of the best. Ask Allah to grant us the sweetness of looking at Him (s.w.t.). Therefore recite the following *du'a'* of the Prophet Muḥammad (s.a.w.)—to ask Allah for the sweetness of looking at Him (s.w.t.):

اللَّهُمَّ بِعِلْمِكَ الْغَيْبَ وَقُدْرَتِكَ عَلَى الْخَلْقِ أَحْيِنِي مَا عَلِمْتَ الْحَيَاةَ خَيْرًا لِي وَتَوَفَّنِي إِذَا عَلِمْتَ الْوَفَاةَ خَيْرًا لِي اللَّهُمَّ وَأَسْأَلُكَ خَشْيَتَكَ فِي الْغَيْبِ وَالشَّهَادَةِ وَأَسْأَلُكَ كَلِمَةَ الْحَقِّ فِي الرِّضَا وَالْغَضَبِ وَأَسْأَلُكَ الْقَصْدَ فِي الْفَقْرِ وَالْغِنَى وَأَسْأَلُكَ نَعِيمًا لاَ يَنْفَدُ وَأَسْأَلُكَ قُرَّةَ عَيْنٍ لاَ تَنْقَطِعُ وَأَسْأَلُكَ الرِّضَاءَ بَعْدَ الْقَضَاءِ وَأَسْأَلُكَ بَرْدَ الْعَيْشِ بَعْدَ الْمَوْتِ وَأَسْأَلُكَ لَذَّةَ النَّظَرِ إِلَى

وَجْهِكَ وَالشَّوْقَ إِلَـى لِقَائِكَ فِـي غَيْرِ ضَرَّاءَ مُضِرَّةٍ وَلاَ فِتْنَةٍ مُضِلَّةٍ اللَّهُمَّ زَيِّنَّا بِزِينَـةِ الإِيمَـانِ وَاجْعَلْنَـا هُـدَاةً مُهْتَدِيـنَ

"Allāhumma bi'ilmikal-ghaiba wa qudratika 'alal-khalqi ahyinī mā 'alimtal-ḥayāta khairan lī watawaffanī idhā 'alimtal-wafāta khairan lī, Allāhumma wa as'aluka khashyataka fil-ghaibi wash-shahādah wa as'aluka kalimatal-ḥaqqi fir-riḍā wal-ghaḍab wa as'alukal-qaṣda fil-faqri wal-ghinā wa as'aluka na'īman la yanfad wa as'aluka qurrata 'aynin lā tanqaṭi' wa as'alukar-riḍā'a ba'dal-qaḍā' wa as'aluka bardal-'aishi ba'dal-maut wa as'aluka ladhdhatan-naẓari ila wajhika wash-shauqa ila liqā'ika fī ghairi ḍarrā'a muḍirrah, wa lā fitnatin muḍillah, Allāhumma zayyinnā bizīnatil-īmān waj'alnā hudātan muhtadīn."

"O' Allah, by Your knowledge of the unseen and Your power over creation, keep me alive so long as You know that living is good for me and cause me to die when You know that death is better for me. O' Allah, cause me to fear You in secret and in public. I ask You to make me true in speech in times of pleasure and of anger. I ask You to make me moderate in times of wealth and poverty. And I ask You for everlasting delight and joy that will never cease. I ask You to make me pleased with that which You have decreed and for an easy life after death. I ask You for the sweetness of looking upon Your face and a longing to meet You in a manner that does not entail a calamity that will bring about harm or a trial that will cause deviation. O' Allah, beautify us with the adornment of faith and make us among those who guide and are rightly guided."

(Sunan an-Nasa'i 1305)

Whoever loves to meet Allah, Allah loves to meet him.

And whoever looks forward to meet Allah, Allah looks forward to meeting him.

CHAPTER 25

Seeking Allah's Forgiveness

Dear brothers and sisters, another step we must take to enter *Jannah* and meet Allah—other than reading the aforementioned *du'a's*—is by seeking Allah the Almighty's forgiveness.

We must seek Allah's forgiveness every day. It is one of the most beautiful and quickest ways of getting into *Jannah*. Therefore, constantly seek the forgiveness of Allah.

We are all human beings. There are things that we have done in life that we are embarrassed about, including myself. I too wish I could return in time and not do those things. However, I am just a human. I sometimes end up doing things that I am not happy with.

Laziness often overtakes us. Human nature often overtakes us. And so, we need to seek the forgiveness of Allah for the sins that we have done—for the sins that we remember and the sins we have forgotten.

Supplicate to Allah and ask for His forgiveness, "O' Allah, you know the sins that I have committed—sins that I remember and that which I do not. O' Allah, forgive me for committing those sins. Forgive me for all of them. I love you, O' Allah. I have never sinned out of defiance to you. I have only sinned out of human nature by the trap of my own *nafs* and the trap of *shaytan*." The Prophet (s.a.w.) used to supplicate the following *du'a'*:

اللَّهُمَّ اغْفِرْ لِي خَطِيئَتِي وَجَهْلِي
وَإِسْرَافِي فِي أَمْرِي وَمَا أَنْتَ أَعْلَمُ بِهِ
مِنِّي اللَّهُمَّ اغْفِرْ لِي جِدِّي وَهَزْلِي
وَخَطَئِي وَعَمْدِي وَكُلُّ ذَلِكَ عِنْدِي
اللَّهُمَّ اغْفِرْ لِي مَا قَدَّمْتُ وَمَا أَخَّرْتُ
وَمَا أَسْرَرْتُ وَمَا أَعْلَنْتُ وَمَا أَنْتَ أَعْلَمُ

$$\text{بِهِ مِنِّي أَنْتَ الْمُقَدِّمُ وَأَنْتَ الْمُؤَخِّرُ}$$
$$\text{وَأَنْتَ عَلَى كُلِّ شَيْءٍ قَدِيرٌ}$$

"Allāhumma-ghfirlī khaṭī'atī wa jahlī wa isrāfī fī 'amrī wa mā anta a'lamu bihi minnī, Allāhumma-ghfirlī jiddī wa hazlī wa khaṭa'ī wa 'amdī wa kullu dhalika 'indī, Allāhumma-ghfirlī mā qaddamtu wa mā akhkhartu wa mā asrartu wa mā a'lantu wa mā Anta a'lamu bihi minnī. Antal-Muqaddim wa Antal-Mu'akhkhir wa Anta 'ala kulli shai'in Qadīr."

"O' Allah, forgive me my faults, my ignorance, my immoderation in my concerns. And Thou art better aware (of my affairs) than myself. O' Allah, grant me forgiveness (of the faults which I committed) seriously or otherwise (and which I committed inadvertently and deliberately. All these (failings) are in me. O' Allah, grant me forgiveness from the fault which I did in haste or deferred, which I committed in privacy or in public and Thou art better aware of (them) than myself. Thou art the First and the Last and over all things Thou art Omnipotent."

(Ṣaḥīḥ Muslim 2719a)

In essence, seek Allah's forgiveness. If the Prophet (s.a.w.) sought Allah's forgiveness seventy to a hundred times every day even though he (s.a.w.) did not need it, then it is only for us to replicate and follow it, because we need it.

Those who constantly **seek Allah's forgiveness**,

Allah will **appoint** for him **a way out** of every distress,

and a **relief** from every **anxiety**,

and will provide **sustenance** for him from where **he expects not**.

CHAPTER 26

Improving Ourselves

After seeking Allah's forgiveness, strive for the betterment of and strengthen ourselves. Improve ourselves. Be strong. Allah will make it happen, *inshā'Allāh*.

Improve little by little every day.

Improve one thing every day.

Human nature can make us falter but we can always improve. Improve our prayer and our dress codes—and this is for both men and women. Some of the dress codes are just so ridiculous. The men are wearing trousers that are almost at the knee. And so when they are praying, they are pulling it down.

Astagfirullāh. We are in the house of Allah and these incidents happen.

Do we really reckon people like this will be going to the right place in the Hereafter? Do we really think we will be seeing those men who were wearing short pants sitting and chilling in *Jannah*? No. It is not going to happen. Therefore, we should better ourselves and behave like a true believer would. Please dear brothers and sisters, behave in this way.

And so, when we talk about dress codes, I am not only speaking about the sisters, but also the brothers as well. Both need to improve. And we should also improve ourselves by connecting to Allah and the Qur'an. Read at least one verse every day. Is it too much to read just one verse? No. Do this and our life will change before we even know it. At one point, we will start doing two verses, and then three verses, and then more, *inshā'Allāh*. However, we need to make the effort so that when we meet Allah, we can present Him with these deeds—good deeds and good secret deeds that are only between us and Allah.

A believer who recites the Qur'an is like a citron,

whose fragrance is sweet and whose taste is sweet.

A believer who does not recite the Qur'an is like a date,

which has no fragrance but has a sweet taste.

A hypocrite who recites the Qur'an is like basil,

whose fragrance is sweet but whose taste is bitter.

A hypocrite who does not recite the Qur'an is like the colocynth,

which has neither fragrance nor sweetness, and only bitterness.

CHAPTER 27

Staying Connected to Allah

Dear brothers and sisters, when we—may Allah the Almighty protect us—commit sins, do not do it openly. Why? Because we are believers.

It is mentioned in the following hadith that people will remain in goodness as long as they do not openly, arrogantly and proudly commit sins:

Narrated Abu Hurayrah:

I heard Allah's Messenger (s.a.w.) saying: "All the sins of my followers will be forgiven except those of the Mujahirin (those who commit a sin openly or disclose their sins to the people). An example of such disclosure is that a person commits a sin at night and though Allah screens it from the public, then he comes in the morning, and says, 'O' so-and-so, I did such-and-such (evil) deed yesterday,' though he spent his night screened by his Lord (none knowing about his sin) and in the morning he removes Allah's screen from himself."

(Ṣaḥīḥ al-Bukhari 6069)

When we commit a sin and advertise it to everyone—it is a terrible thing.

However, if we have done it privately and quietly, and we are embarrassed about our actions, that means we are still believers. I am not saying it is okay to sin. The main essence is that we should try our best not to sin. However, if we falter and end up committing a sin, make sure it is private as it shows that we are embarrassed. Hence, we still have some form of connection with Allah, which is why we did a private sin and not a public sin.

In the same way, we want our sins to be private, do some good deeds in private as well. Have private good deeds that are just between us and Allah. Deeds that no one else knows. This is so that when we get to the Hereafter, we have some hidden deeds between us and Allah. For instance, getting up once in a while for *tahajjud* to pray and cry to Allah. Perhaps once in a while, we can do that. *Tahajjud* is not compulsory but it is a very good deed.

Other examples could be perhaps helping and assisting someone for the sake of Allah. However, it is done quietly. We are helping people, widows, orphans, homeless people or some downtrodden people but it is done quietly. We do deeds quietly and no one knows about it except Allah.

In essence, we should keep some silent deeds. I know a few people who after they have passed away, their silent deeds are brought to light. It was found that they used to help so many people, they were charitable and so on. *Mashā'Allāh*. Their deeds surfaced after their deaths. *SubḥānAllāh*. Good news to these people. May Allah the Almighty grant us goodness. I pray that Allah the Almighty looks forward to meeting us the same way we look forward to meeting Him. And I pray that Allah will grant us all His forgiveness.

And whoever commits a good deed, We will increase for him good therein. Indeed, Allah is Forgiving and Appreciative.

Ending Remarks

Before we end, I would like to tell all the readers that, *inshā'Allāh*, we will all be going to *Jannah*. We have to. We refuse to go elsewhere. The Prophet (s.a.w.) mentioned in a hadith:

Narrated Abu Hurayrah:

> Allah's Messenger (s.a.w.) said, "All my followers will enter Paradise except those who refuse." They said, "O' Allah's Messenger (s.a.w.)! Who will refuse?" He said, "Whoever obeys me will enter Paradise, and whoever disobeys me is the one who refuses (to enter it)."
>
> (Ṣaḥīḥ al-Bukhari 7280)

The Prophet Muḥammad (s.a.w.) mentioned that we will all be going to *Jannah* except the ones who refuse. Who is refusing amongst us, dear readers? No one. We all want to go to *Jannah* and *inshā'Allāh* we are all going to *Jannah*. So have hope in the mercy of Allah.

Ponder this: Have we done good deeds in our lives? If yes, continue to do more and ask Allah to accept them. If we have not, then we try harder and ask Allah to accept them too. Seek Allah's forgiveness for all the bad things we have done. Whoever follows in the path of Allah (s.w.t.) and His Messenger (s.a.w.), will, *inshā'Allāh*, go to *Jannah*. Try our best.

Do not forget as well that we are all human beings; we might falter, but then seek forgiveness and improve ourselves. Some people become too hard on themselves, that they start struggling with different types of OCD and so on. We are too hard on ourselves then. We strive to be perfect, we strive for perfection in this world but we cannot. Why? Because we are just human beings.

We can falter, we can forget and sometimes, we might be lazy and perhaps sometimes, fall into sin. However, when that happens, seek forgiveness from Allah the Almighty. That is what makes us a believer. We try to improve and try our best to not go back to the wrong path so that we will all enter *Jannah* by the will of Allah.

In essence, remember what I have taught throughout the book: Focus on **getting** to *Jannah* more than focusing on what we **will have and want** there. Basically, do not worry about what we will have in *Jannah*. *Inshā'Allāh* when we get there, we will know. At the same time, I do not mean not to think about it at all. Sometimes we can think about it, there is no harm. The Qur'an and hadith have mentioned the description of *Jannah*. However, the main focus and priority should be getting there. Do not create a wish list of things that we want and then lose our focus, lose ourselves. Do not lose focus and end up somewhere else.

Let me give an example: We are planning to go on a holiday to Japan and so we wrote a list of all the things we want to do. However, we have mistakenly jumped on an aeroplane to Nigeria, which is also, *mashā'Allāh*, a very beautiful place. But the list that we did is filled with Japanese things and foods and places. So how are we going to find all those things in Nigeria? We ended up in that state because we were writing a list for the wrong place. We were so worried about what we wanted, that we lost focus on the fact that the ticket was actually for going somewhere else. That is the example of a person who is worried about what he wants, and then loses focus. When we lose focus, we might not end up in *Jannah*.

May Allah make it easy for us. May Allah give us the strength to always be focused on His ultimate path. May we all be granted the chance to meet our Creator—Allah the Almighty.

Whoever makes the Hereafter his goal, Allah makes his heart rich, and organises his affairs, and the world comes to him whether it wants to or not.

And whoever makes the world his goal, Allah puts his poverty right before his eyes, and disorganises his affairs, and the world does not come to him, except what has been decreed for him.

Arabic Glossary

Akhirah - The Hereafter

Alhamdulillāh - Praise be to Allah

Allāhu Akbar - Allah is the Greatest

Astagfirullāh - I seek forgiveness in Allah

Ayah - Verse

Deen - Religion

Dhikr - Remembrance to Allah

Du'a' - Prayer

Dunya - Worldly

Hajj - Pilgrimage

'Illiyyun - The seventh Heaven

Iman - Faith

Inshā'Allāh - If Allah wills

Jahannam - Hellfire

Jannah - Heaven

Jinn - Demons

Lā ʾilāha ʾillā-llāh - There is no god but Allah

Maghrib - Sunset prayer, one of the five mandatory *ṣalah* (Islamic prayer)

Malaʾikah of *maut* - Angel of death

MashāʾAllāh - As Allah has willed

Mawaddah - Compassion

Mizan - Scale for weighing deeds

Nafs - Self

Raḥmah - Mercy

Ṣabr - Patience

Ṣadaqah - Charity

aṣ-Ṣadiqin - The truthful ones

Ṣalah - Prayer

Shahadah - Testimony

Shayṭan - Devil

Sijjin - An eternal prison beneath the seventh earth

SubḥānAllāh - Glory be to Allah

Tahajjud - Night prayer

Tarawiḥ - Sunnah prayer performed during Ramadan

Wallāhi - I swear to Allah

Zakah - Almsgiving

www.ingramcontent.com/pod-product-compliance
Lightning Source LLC
LaVergne TN
LVHW061344080526
838199LV00094B/7273